Alfred Jarry

Titles in the series Critical Lives present the work of leading cultural figures of the modern period. Each book explores the life of the artist, writer, philosopher or architect in question and relates it to their major works.

Alfred Jarry

Jill Fell

REAKTION BOOKS

In memory of Barbara Wright

Published by Reaktion Books Ltd
33 Great Sutton Street
London EC1V 0DX, UK

www.reaktionbooks.co.uk

First published 2010

Printed and bound in Great Britain
by CPI /Antony Rowe, Chippenham, Wiltshire

British Library Cataloguing in Publication Data
Fell, Jill, 1947–
    Alfred Jarry. – (Critical lives)
    1. Jarry, Alfred, 1873–1907 – Criticism and interpretation
    I. Title II. Series
    842.8-DC22

ISBN: 978 1 86189 755 8

Contents

Prologue

The bronze statue (see overleaf) of Alfred Jarry that stands in the town square of his birthplace, Laval, shows him with his two most important possessions: his racing bicycle and his Bulldog revolver. The sculptor, Ossip Zadkine, has moulded them to his body. Shooting episodes, real or invented, punctuate Jarry's life story. Varying versions of the same event present a problem for the biographer. Jarry's behaviour made such a strong impression on the young André Gide that he later placed him among the fictitious characters of his novel *The Counterfeiters*. Gide perceived that the tiny writer, with his clown-white face and violent antics, had belonged more to the world of fiction than to the real one:

> In traditional circus clown's clothes, everything about Jarry seemed affected; especially his way of speaking, that others often imitated … hammering out each syllable, inventing bizarre words, strangely deforming others; but only Jarry himself could achieve the utter flatness of voice, with no warmth, intonation or relief.
>
> When you get to know him, I assure you he's charming, said Olivier.
>
> I'd rather not. He has a violent look about him.
>
> He puts it on. Passavant thinks he's very gentle in reality. But he's drunk a huge amount this evening; and not a drop of water, would you believe; nor wine: nothing but absinthe and

strong liqueurs. Passavant is worried that he'll do something eccentric.[1]

At this point in the story Jarry is heard to mutter 'And now we're going to kill little Bercail.' The person in question challenges him to repeat his threat more loudly, which he does, drawing a large pistol out of his pocket and twirling it. Bercail now stands on a chair to show that he is not afraid. Jarry does the same and takes aim. Someone turns out the lights. A shot is heard, but the pistol only has blanks in it. When the lights go on Bercail is seen to be still standing on his chair.

At the actual dinner of 1897 that Gide fictionalized, Jarry had hit his victim with his bare fists. No shots were fired on that occasion, but Gide probably combined it with a later real shooting incident. A dramatic episode in 1905, when Jarry did shoot at a fellow dinner guest, has been depicted by three other writers, whose recollections are all different. What is unclear from the three accounts is whether Picasso, who later denied having known Jarry, took over his gun at or after the dinner at which the shooting took place. He may not even have been present.

The host of the 1905 dinner was Maurice Raynal, a young poet who entertained well, and who had a great affection for Jarry. His account was not written until twenty-eight years after the event:

> That evening several friends had got together at my little place in the rue de Rennes. Among these were Apollinaire, Maurice Cremnitz, Picasso, André Salmon, Manolo, Max Jacob, Alfred Jarry and three young women who were all expecting, I think. The dinner had been quite lively. A hunting friend had sent me some magnificent wild duck, which were the *pièces de résistance* of the dinner. When they were put on the table, Jarry offered his services. 'I'm an expert at carving these birds,' he said, then grasped the birds with both hands and tore them to pieces.

Ossip Zadkine, Preliminary plaster model for a statue of Alfred Jarry, 1938.

All the guests except for the Spanish sculptor, Manolo, were indulging heavily in the excellent Beaujolais provided by their wealthy young host. Raynal relates that Manolo soon remained the only guest who was not drunk. The sculptor's quiet, sober presence began to get on Jarry's nerves and he began to shout at him to leave. Jarry's demands became more and more insistent until he finally yelled 'If your Manolo doesn't get out, I'm going to kill him.'

> Out of his pocket he all at once produced a foul rusty little Bulldog revolver. Greasy as an old wallet, it had no shine on it and I assumed that it was fortunately in too bad a state to work, the idiot, when suddenly he brandished it in the air and fired two shots at Manolo.[2]

Raynal contradicts Apollinaire's account of 1909 that the shots had caused consternation and caused two of the pregnant women (one of whom was his wife) to faint. He claims that nobody took any notice!

Apollinaire's account has the virtue of relative immediacy. It was written within four years of the actual event, instead of nearly three decades. Of the three chronicles of the evening, his is the only one to omit Picasso. In his narrative there is, however, an artist friend whom he elects not to name, in whose atelier he says the Bulldog revolver stayed for six months. He goes on to give his account of the dinner:

> We had been invited to a dinner in the rue de Rennes. During dinner, someone having wanted to read his hand, Jarry proved that all his lines were double. To show how strong he was, he turned the plates over and broke them with his fists, ending up by injuring himself. The aperitifs and wine had gone to his head. The liqueurs were the last straw. A Spanish sculptor wanted to introduce himself and was politely complimenting

him. But Jarry ordered this *bouffre* to get out and not come back again, assuring me that the fellow had just made him some disgraceful proposals. After a few minutes the Spaniard came back and Jarry immediately fired a shot at him. The bullet embedded itself in a curtain. Two pregnant women who were present fainted. Nor were the men happy with the situation and two of us took Jarry out. In the road he told me in Père Ubu's voice: 'Wasn't that just beautiful as literature? But I forgot to pay for the drinks.'

As we took him out we disarmed him, and six months later he came to Montmartre to reclaim the revolver that our friend had forgotten to give back to him.[3]

In his memoir, Apollinaire implies that the revolver was out of Jarry's possession from April to the end of October 1905. To Jarry's knowledge it was Apollinaire who had taken charge of the gun and, in a letter of 22 April, a few days after the dinner, he asked for it back within the week, holding him responsible for its safe-keeping.[4] Yet Apollinaire's friend had obviously persuaded Apollinaire to let him take it. If the forgetful friend had been Picasso, would Apollinaire have named him in his memoir of Jarry and risked embarrassing him? The fact that Jarry apparently had to go to Montmartre to reclaim his gun after so long did not reflect well on the friend concerned.

Max Jacob wrote two versions of the dinner; the published account is less detailed than his draft, in which he claimed that he and Picasso went to Raynal's together:

Picasso and Jarry took to each other immediately and stayed friends thereafter, without seeing each other very much . . . I remember having been drunk . . . and, after regrettably falling asleep on the stair carpet, I was woken by shots from a revolver. Jarry was yelling 'Death to the buggers!' or 'Out with the buggers!' The following day I learnt that he was after Manolo! . . . Well, this was the revolver that became Picasso's. Jarry gave it to him. It is possible that Picasso has it still, for from that moment on he was never parted from it.[5]

The Picasso expert Pierre Daix claims that there has never been any question of either Jacob or Picasso having been at Raynal's dinner.[6] Picasso's denial of having known Jarry, confided to his friend, Hélène Parmelin, is currently the accepted one:

He said that he regretted not having known Jarry; that he had gone to see him one day with Apollinaire, but Jarry was out and then it was all over. He died.[7]

1

Laval, Saint-Brieuc and Rennes

Jarry was never to attain old age. He thought he would die at 33, the same age as Christ, but past his prime by 29 and consuming daily quantities of alcohol sufficient to kill much larger men, he just achieved the age of 34. Poet, artist, dramatist, novelist and journalist, he concentrated his main creative effort into a mere ten years, 1893–1903.

For an insight into Jarry's early years we are thrown back on the fragmentary and chronologically chaotic notes written after his death by his sister, Charlotte. Eight years his senior, Charlotte played a large part in looking after the young Alfred, a role that she had to pick up again when he constantly returned to convalesce in her care during his last years. Although the records of their vast orders of wine imply that her consumption of alcohol may not have been far behind her brother's at this time, Charlotte's constitution must have been the stronger. Ultimately impoverished like him, she nevertheless lived to 60 years of age.

Alfred-Henri Jarry was born on 8 September 1873 to Anselme and Caroline Jarry in the northern town of Laval on the River Mayenne, close to the Breton border. To Charlotte we owe the facts that Caroline boasted a head of magnificent 'nearly-blonde' curls and Anselme a neat dark beard.[1] When, in the summer of 1863, Caroline's father, Judge Charles Quernest, had given her away in marriage at the age of twenty, it had been to a solid business-man with prospects. It may have been a relief to get a wilful and headstrong daughter settled and materially secure, even though the Jarry family did not have the same social and intellectual standing as the Quernests. In 1867, when Charlotte was a toddler of two and a half, Anselme's textiles business was doing well enough for him to move his family out of his mother's house, 13 rue de Bootz, across the river to the more fashionable old town in the shadow of Laval castle. Charlotte recalled that her parents had planted a flower garden, complete with landscaped pond and installed an aviary with a large selection of birds.[2]

Between the birth of Charlotte and Alfred, the Jarrys lost a baby boy, who had only survived for two weeks. This loss made the subsequent arrival of Alfred and his early care a joyful and yet anxious business. Charlotte remembers receiving detailed instructions from her grandfather by letter, on how to encourage her little brother's development. The signs are that Judge Quernest, whose own son was socially maladjusted and an alcoholic, invested all his hopes in his grandson. Charlotte's role in the affair of Alfred's upbringing was spelt out to her from an early age. Her small importance to her parents is underlined by their neglect of her baptism until just before that of her brother's, which took place a mere month after his birth. Although only nine years old herself, Charlotte was given the additional responsibility of being god-mother to this much desired son.

In a strangely unimaginative and ambitious move Anselme had a large family house built back in rue de Bootz. What had been a steep but short walk to and from the children's school every morning would now involve a much more inconvenient journey across the river and the separation of his son from his playmates, as well as of his wife from her friends, the other school mothers. These included a certain Madame Locré. Charlotte recalls a picnic excursion that her mother and Alfred, aged three, had undertaken with Madame Locré and her daughter, Jeanne, aged four. While the young mothers were absorbed in their conversation, the unsupervised children happily consumed the cakes and most of a bottle of wine. They had to be drenched in cold water, writes Charlotte, to bring them back to consciousness.[3] Unfortunately we know nothing of the future life of Jarry's first girlfriend and drinking partner.

Caroline believed she was descended from an ancient line of Breton aristocracy, and, through her family name, Coutouly de Dorset, from the Dukes of Dorset.[4] She may have felt that she had married beneath herself. Jarry later claimed that she had been the despair of her husband.[5] If there was strain in the marriage, it became much worse in 1879 when Anselme's business foundered, apparently due to the negligence of his partner, in whose hands he had left it while he was travelling. In the attempt to clear his debts his mother sold one of her houses and his wife's dowry was forfeited. Here he was, suddenly forced to declare bankruptcy, with no choice but to fall back on his previous job as a commercial traveller. He was 42, Caroline 36. The school fees for the children could no longer be covered. Charlotte relates that her mother refused a scholarship for them, which would have represented social humiliation.[6] Indeed it would have been difficult for Caroline to keep up appearances in Laval at all. She moved abruptly with her teenage daughter and six-year-old son to the security of her childhood home on the Brittany coast. Caroline had argued for the move on the grounds of the children's health, as Charlotte later wrote: 'The plaster in the new house made us cough. We went to live in Saint-Brieuc near grandfather, Justice of the Peace.'[7]

Caroline's mother, Octavie Sophronie Coutouly, had already been in a mental asylum for years, leaving her father with no presiding female to keep an eye on his domestic affairs. Given that Anselme's absences would now be frequent, she could explain the decision in terms of sheer filial duty. Her father, a well-to-do local magistrate, would provide a stable paternal authority and role model for the young Alfred, as well as lending her a status that her husband could no longer provide. Anselme nevertheless continued to support his wife and family whether in Saint-Brieuc, Rennes or finally Paris. Indeed the address of the two-storey house where she lived for nine years in Saint-Brieuc was given as the absent spouse's main residence.[8] Latterly the need for mother and son to rent not one but two apartments and keep up appearances in the capital city must have been an increasing drain on Anselme's finances. Jarry's alleged dismissive comment about his father, that he was 'an insignificant little fellow, what you would call a thoroughly good chap',[9] glosses over what seems to have been a healthy relationship during his teens. As soon as Alfred was old enough to travel to Laval by himself, he combined competing in sporting events such as cycling, fencing and shooting with visits to his father.[10] The rift between them was caused by a later incident.

Memories of school played an abnormally vivid part in the psyche of this writer. For a start, no other schoolmaster can have achieved the mythical status and notoriety conferred on the physics teacher, Félix Hébert, through his transformation into the monster Ubu by his former pupil. Even Jarry's first teacher at his little school by the Laval castle is immortalized. A strict and demanding figure, she appears in Jarry's novel *L'amour absolu* as Madame Venelle, wielding the indispensable teacher's aid of the time, 'akin to a fairy's wand'. The actual instrument used for rapping pupils' knuckles was not, however, a ruler but the white, probably ivory, handle of her paper knife.[11] The exacting teacher, whose real name was Madame Venel, must have earned the five-year-old's respect, for in 1878 she included Jarry among the pupils who deserved a reward for both application and behaviour.[12] In *L'amour absolu* Jarry tells the story through Emmanuel, his fictional self. The paper knife becomes an instrument of power in his imagination and he persuades his father to carve him some of these sword substitutes, then decorating them himself. It seems that Jarry developed his talent for carving very young. However, this early artistic cooperation between father and son was to be cut short.

Anselme Jarry was now left to a grim routine of commercial travelling. Apart from his son's occasional visits, he would return to an empty house. He was none the less committed to supporting his young wife and family. Caroline meanwhile turned her back on her marriage of sixteen years in her determination to restore her own situation and to give her adored son the best opportunities within her power. Her anxieties for his health would eventually lead to her own death.

The move to Saint-Brieuc would have been much more difficult for the thirteen-year-old Charlotte than for her small brother. Not particularly attractive, nor a strong personality, the sudden separation from the school friends of a lifetime would have been hard to bear; while at five, the age of her little brother, memories are short and new friends are easily made. Now began the most stable period of Jarry's life and perhaps the happiest – nine years in a pretty seaside village, with unbroken schooling, the beach as his playground and the loving attention of grandfather, mother and sister.

From October 1879 until the end of the school year of 1888 Alfred was a pupil at the Lycée de Saint-Brieuc. He seems to have been a model student, usually near the top of his form and winner of several prizes in his last three years. Between the ages of twelve and sixteen he also took to writing small poems and plays in his spare time. It was quite usual for schoolchildren of this period and even well into the twentieth century to be set the task of writing poems modelled on those of famous poets. What is unusual is that, in adulthood, Jarry recopied, dated and preserved all the early pieces that he had written in his teens, naming the collection *Ontogénie,* a biological term which pertains to the origin and development of an individual living being from birth to adulthood. Certain of the future importance of his work, he wanted his early efforts to be available to scholars. They were found at the back of a drawer at the offices of his publisher, the Mercure de France, in 1947, where they had lain since his death.

Almost all Jarry's early poems take an existing poem, picture or famous quotation as their springboard. A fierce antipathy to tyranny, cruelty and hypocrisy already governs his choices. The germ of the future *Ubu Roi* is present in a tyrant king, who frivolously forces a condemned man to put on his crown and hold his sceptre before executing him.[13] The young poet sees to it that these tyrant figures get their comeuppance.

In maturity the vogue for *transposition d'art* encouraged Jarry to continue the habit of using a picture to inspire a poem. Poetry did not come naturally to him. Neither the child nor the man possessed the inner lyrical impulse of say, Arthur Rimbaud, and in which Rimbaud's much harsher upbringing probably played a role. In childhood Jarry did not need an escape route from his material lot. Sacrifices would be made to give the two Jarry children every educational advantage: piano lessons for Charlotte and private tuition in both English and German for Alfred. This tuition would ease his friendships with the English artists and writers whom he later met and stand him in good stead for the translations he undertook.

Charlotte writes how her small brother used to go in search of ponds and pools, to find insects and pursue butterflies with the seriousness of an adult naturalist.[14] He seems to have been allowed to run fairly wild, and these childhood experiences became not only a part of his imaginative resource, but the Breton backcloth to his later novels. There he evokes 'freshwater springs so close to the sea that the water was prickly with crabs and pond creatures'[15] and chasing crickets, even blocking up the holes into which they fled.[16]

This happy existence was brought to an end once again by his ambitious mother. Saint-Brieuc was too small to give Alfred the education that his academic potential deserved, in her view. The Lycée in Rennes, capital of Brittany, would provide the teaching and the competition that would stretch her son's capabilities. Domestic upheaval never deterred Caroline Jarry in pursuit of this aim. No wonder Jarry never lost the inner conviction that his work would be valued by posterity. Charlotte, now 22, already two years older than her mother had been at her marriage, came along too.

The Lycée de Rennes would provide the most important and formative encounter of Jarry's life. He could not have foreseen that the master who there became the butt of his mockery would be the catalyst to releasing his creative powers and setting the course of his life. Most of the masters at the Lycée were in their early thirties. At 56, the physics master, Félix Hébert, was a ponderous figure by comparison. This was the man who would become the model for Jarry's Ubu. Only by teaching could Hébert support his passion for meteorology, the subject of his doctoral thesis, but teaching was clearly not his métier. His first inspector's report from Rennes was bad:

> Mr Hébert's delivery is slow and muddled. His lessons lack clarity and coordination. Next to nothing is retained by the pupils. He has no idea how to impose his authority or to engage the slightest amount of attention from his pupils. The discipline problems with the sixth class reached such a low point that the censor was forced to remove him from this class.

By the end of the 1888–9 academic year, Jarry's first, the inspector's concern about Monsieur Hébert had deepened to one of alarm for the reputation of the school itself:

> From his very first days here, his arrival in the classroom has been greeted with mocking chants and, since then, we have seen a repetition of the problems that I pointed out to you previously. Shouting, murmuring, grotesque antics by the pupils; total inability by the teacher to make himself heard, leading to claims

against the school and bitter complaints from families, rightly concerned about the adverse consequences this kind of situation could have on their sons, both now and in the future.[17]

Pandemonium ruled in Hébert's classes. Looking back, one of Jarry's classmates, Henri Hertz, remembers the unfortunate master, his coat tails dangling like an insect's wings, back turned to the boys and clinging to the blackboard like a vast fly to a windowpane. The master's enormous paunch was supported by two very short legs on flat feet. Tiny eyes peeped out from his fleshy face. Hairy fingers fiddled nervously with his goatee beard.[18] His yellowing moustache has been immortalized by the painters of the two surviving Ubu puppets. Jarry's verbal attacks were so accomplished that his classmates made silence for them. Any unaccustomed silence in this class was merely the prelude to a particularly cruel barrage of questions from the merciless teenager, whose aim was to reduce the old master to a state of collapse, if not tears. Hertz uses the term *maieutic* of Jarry's speaking style, a method developed by Socrates to release latent concepts in the mind. A future schoolmate in Paris who was present at Jarry's initiation address for the Lycée Henri IV recalled him giving a similar pyrotechnical display of apparent intellect. Possessed of a penetrating voice, according to Hertz, Jarry clearly began rehearsing his rhetorical technique early.

The other teachers acknowledged the excellence of Jarry's academic work without wanting to hold it up as an example. Pupils and teachers alike recognized that there was something worryingly different about the boy. Evoking Jarry's mixture of intellect and pugnacity, Hertz describes his butting forehead as hewn like an ancient ballistic missile. He also refers to Jarry's 'bizarre' reading tastes. Nicknamed Quasimodo on account of his bandy legs and lack of height, he made an intimidating impact with the disconcerting seriousness of his verbal assaults, delivered in a peculiar rasping voice.

Félix Hébert, Jarry's physics teacher.

The anecdotes that have built the Jarry myth begin here. Charlotte writes, no doubt reliably, of her brother studying in bed from five o'clock in the morning, surrounded by dictionaries and keeping himself going with coffee. He already decorates his room with skeletons that bob in the moonlight and possesses a guitar as well as a bicycle. He has also taken up shooting at a local gallery.[19] A school friend tells a tale of him arriving at school looking as if he had not been to bed, his shoes wet and muddy, his collar undone. Asked for an explanation, his rasping staccato voice delivered the riposte: 'I've come dir...ect...ly...from...the...broth...els.'[20]

The baiting of Monsieur Hébert drew Jarry into close friendship with his classmate Henri Morin and into the momentous collaborative effort that would lead to his future fame. Henri had already collaborated with his brother Charles, three years older, in the compiling of a play titled *Les Polonais,* celebrating the fictitious adventures of Père Hébert, whose name over the years had suffered many metamorphoses from the simple Père Eb to P.H., Ébon, Ébance, Ébouille. The drawings with which the Morin brothers filled the margins of their scripts fixed the caricatural outline of Père Hébert, to which Jarry, and later Pierre Bonnard, adhered. When Jarry renamed the play *Ubu Roi* he retained *Les Polonais* as the alternative title. The siting of the play in Poland, not a state at the time, meant that the action took place in a fictitious setting like *Erewhon.* By Jarry's own account in *La Critique*, the choice of Poland (La Pologne) was based on a linguistic construct, combining the Greek *pou*, a vague interrogative adverb of place, with the French *loin*, meaning 'far away'.[21] Jarry had written: 'The action takes place in Poland, a country both dismembered and legendary enough to be this Nowhere, or at the very least, if we take account of a likely Franco-Greek etymology, a far away interrogative somewhere.'[22]

A more recent speculation points out that chamber pots were popularly known as *polonais* or 'Polish buckets' and argues that this would fit in with the lavatorial humour of the Rennes creative inspiration.[23] Jarry's characters, Jean Sobieski, General Lascy, Stanislas Leczinski and Nicolas Rensky, are all genuine historical figures. It is quite possible that Louis Lemercier de Neuville's illustrated, historical work on famous Polish military figures, *Galerie polonaise* of 1863, which glorified 'the flower of Polish nobility' pitted against 'the infamous Russian fur hats' in the uprising of that year, was known to the boys from history lessons or family libraries and had a bearing on both their choice of title and the plot of the play. Lemercier de Neuville (1830–1918), better known for his writing on marionettes and a native of Laval, would certainly have been known to Jarry as Laval's most famous living citizen.

Charlotte's brief notes provide an important chronicle of the early productions of *Les Polonais* by the so-called Théâtre des

Phynances. The play, first shown in the Morins' attic, was enacted in different forms: first with live actors, then as a shadow play and finally with actual puppets. Charlotte was responsible for the costumes and for sculpting the first head of Père Hébert, who passed their house every day on his way to the school. Jarry also used the opportunity to produce an oil portrait of Père Hébert hatted and coated. This is one of four oils on wood panels by his hand known to exist. Charlotte includes the interesting detail that Alice, the Héberts' daughter, was 'resplendent in blue silk' at one of the productions.[24] As she is mentioned in the same breath as a bear and a witch, opinions differ as to whether Charlotte meant that she attended in person, or was represented as a marionette. At twenty, she was only three years younger than Charlotte. As neighbours, they may well have become friends despite Alfred's

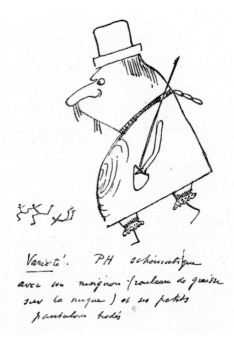

Charles Morin, *Père Hébert*, a sketch from memory made in 1920.

Charlotte Jarry, *c.* 1890.

verbal attacks on Alice's father in class. Charlotte's practical
contribution was certainly very welcome, for the Morin brothers
found the manufacture of the puppets a chore. For them the
shadow theatre held more appeal. Jarry himself was not daunted
by the physical business of marionette manufacture. A letter from
the painter, Henri Rousseau, his Lavallois compatriot, attests to
the existence of a box of his marionettes in 1894, well in advance
of the surviving marionette of Ubu, dated to 1897.[25]

Neither Jarry's extra-curricular activities, nor his indiscipline
within class affected his baccalaureate results. He obtained the

second half with *mention bien*, a mark good enough for his parents to agree that he would be a suitable candidate for the École Normale Supérieure. Anselme applied for special permission for his son to take the examination early. In June 1891, full of hope, Caroline Jarry duly left for Paris with the seventeen-year-old Alfred to sit the entrance examination. It must have been quite a disappointment when Jarry failed to reach the average mark in any of the subjects that he sat for the ENS examination. Mother and son returned swiftly to Rennes without his being admitted to any of the oral examinations.

Jarry's previous year of study, the academic year of 1890–91, was for a long time undocumented. He had stayed on for an extra year at the Lycée de Rennes, in what was known as the Veterans' class, studying for the entrance examination to the Lycée Henri IV in Paris, which would in turn prepare him for the ENS examination. The select few in this class did not have their marks registered in the school records, nor were prizes awarded, which is one of the reasons why Jarry's presence at the school during this year passed unrecorded and why he was long thought to have gone to Paris a year earlier than he actually did. No texts after 8 June 1890 were gathered into the juvenile collection that he titled *Ontogénie*. He clearly believed that, having passed his baccalaureate, he had already crossed the frontier into intellectual maturity. Caroline Jarry had meanwhile set her sights on Paris and on the very best education for her son. Happily, Jarry's efforts in the Veterans' class resulted in his passing the examination that qualified him to enrol in the class of 'Rhétorique supérieure' at the Lycée Henri IV. For the 26-year-old Charlotte this would have been an exciting move and, in her notes about her brother, her exclamation, 'Paris!' seems to indicate that she was included.[26] Caroline duly moved to the capital in October 1891, lodging at 11 rue de Cujas, which, for her son, would involve only a short uphill walk to the Lycée Henri IV.

2

Literary Success and a Rejected Coat

Jarry was impatient to make the transition from schoolboy to adult. He wanted to enter the literary world immediately. During the years 1891–3 he had no financial worries, alcohol had not yet taken hold of his life and his physical and intellectual energy were at their peak. He had studied hard enough to absorb the prodigious knowledge of Greek and Latin required for entry to the *Khâgne* at the Lycée Henri IV, the two-year preparatory class for the École Normale Supérieure examination. He had a reasonable command of English and German and his mastery of mathematics and the sciences was strong enough for him to have considered a career in science. It is fairly obvious that, in his spare time, he concentrated on his literary ambitions to the detriment of his schoolwork. He failed the École Normale Supérieure exam three times when it should have been well within his grasp. According to his sister he did not want to waste any more of his life studying. 'It's bad enough to be at school when you're young', she quotes him as saying.[1]

Whatever his academic performance, Jarry was determined to attain a similar degree of respect and awe from his Parisian classmates as in Rennes. His accent and his family's lack of wealth may have counted against him, but the sophistication of his new audience did not impair his ability to raise a laugh. One particular classmate, Gandilhon Gens-d'Armes, also from the provinces, was himself the victim of Jarry's wit and observed his tormentor's tactics with greater attention than most. By way of an initiation rite, new entrants to the college were given a random subject on which to give an impromptu talk. The subject allocated to Jarry was Turkestan. Here is Gandilhon Gens-d'Armes's account of the way that he tackled it:

'Turkestan! What a bit of luck! A fantastic subject, and the only one that I know in real depth. The Orient, gentlemen, the inexhaustible Orient, etc. etc.' Only a minute had passed before he had already got on to the Turks, Istanbul, Pierre Loti and Aziyadé. He was recalled to the subject. 'The subject?' he said 'but what else do you think I'm talking about? Since when have digressions been forbidden?' . . . He reverted to the subject of Turkestan for a few seconds, but then veered off at full tilt into tortuous, yet faultless sentences on Earthly Paradise, Genghis Khan, Persian poetry, Mahomet II, Saint Sofia, the Suez Canal and anything else that you can possibly imagine. The audience was overwhelmed.[2]

Both Hertz and Gandilhon Gens-d'Armes recall that they were left with the impression of something abnormal, if not satanic, about Jarry's brilliant but chaotic speaking style. Attempting to find a comparison, Gandilhon Gens-d'Armes evoked the disquieting image of a machine driven by a devil. The spectre of the Quernest family's mental instability has to be taken into account as a lurking presence but however disquieting his manner, Jarry was fiercely in control of his galloping mental processes.

Jarry's strange manner did not invite intimacy, but he was disarmed by a sophisticated young man two and half years his junior, who had not even taken his baccalaureate. At seventeen, Léon-Paul Fargue was strikingly good-looking and, with his ruffled hair, a look-alike for Arthur Rimbaud.[3] Fargue enthusiastically introduced his new friend to the artistic and literary geography of the capital. His sympathetic written portrait of the Jarry of their early friendship reveals a less disconcerting personality than Gandilhon Gens-d'Armes's description:

> Alfred Jarry was already an ingenious poet, precise and very much the artist. As a man, he was affectionate and even sentimental. He spoke rapidly in a clear, pleasant voice which as yet had nothing of that affected harshness, of that *Ubuesque* accent, of those attitudes which he was to adopt subsequently. He was in Paris on his own, he often visited my parents' house and we were very fond of him.[4]

Yet Fargue, in later life, refused to answer questions about this friendship. It is said that they were inseparable during the year of 1892–3, until Fargue was sent to Coburg by his father both to improve his German and to put the distractions of Paris out of his reach, including contact with a boy 'much too old for him' in his father's words.[5] Louis Lormel, the editor of *L'Art littéraire*, the magazine to which they both gave their earliest literary contributions, wrote a florid article implying that the relationship was blatantly sexual.[6] He nicknamed Jarry 'The Death's Head' and Fargue 'The Androgyne'. Jarry's first collection seems to record actual incidents in their relationship, both violent and tender, but unambiguously sexual. The title of his play, *Haldernablou*, published in the collection *Les Minutes de Sable Mémorial*, combines Haldern, the Breton version of Alfred, with the name Ablou, after the two protagonists. Fargue had persuaded Jarry to 'debaptize' him from the more explicit original title, *Caméleo*, 'Leo' being too obviously related to 'Léon'. 'Every day we would walk and walk', writes Jarry, 'enlaced in an affectionate embrace, indifferent to the passing hours and the hourglasses, towering like giant ants or mummies, along our way. And his caressing hands on my satin white skin made the green snakes of spasms convulse into life.'[7] Yet the surviving letters from Fargue to Jarry relate to their intellectual interests alone, and the signing off formulae 'serre bien' or 'serre affectueusement la main' betoken nothing more than a normal friendship.[8]

The friendship seems to have ended with a more violent quarrel than usual, after which the two men never spoke to each other again, even if they were in the same company.[9] Interviewed in 1940, Jarry's greatest woman friend, the novelist Rachilde, affirmed that Fargue had admitted to being Jarry's lover. When asked by her what he had done to provoke the scene that led to their break-up, she claimed she had had to beg him to desist from telling her the details.[10] No genuine letters from Jarry to Fargue are known to have survived, but several of Fargue's to Jarry have come to light. Fargue was also among the twenty friends who contributed to Jarry's funeral costs.

In his later writings Fargue was prone to bending the truth. As late as 1927 he even managed to forge a letter purporting to be from Jarry, referring to the poem with which Jarry had won his first literary prize, as a collaborative effort.[11] The Jarry–Fargue friendship was a highly competitive one. Both were trying to publish in one of the small literary magazines and both began by reporting on the avant-garde art exhibitions. They may have deliberately chosen different magazines at first: Fargue *L'Art littéraire* and Jarry *Essais d'art libre.* Jarry then joined *L'Art littéraire*'s contributors, but this honour only came at the cost of a monthly subscription of six francs, a sum that he could then afford much more easily than his younger friend. When it came to contributing to the prestigious *Mercure de France*, literary talent had to be reinforced with a subscription of 100 francs. The allowance which was supposed to be supporting Jarry in his studies was being strewn in the path of his literary ambitions, and not in vain. Alfred Vallette, editor of the *Mercure de France* and his wife, Marguerite Eymery, better known by her *nom de plume* of Rachilde, would become Jarry's most loyal supporters throughout his short life.

Jarry's relationship with the two Vallettes as individuals was very different. Rachilde had already made her name as writer of best-selling scurrilous novels, but although a wife and mother by 1893, and, at 33, thirteen years Jarry's senior, she still cultivated a masculine and somewhat outrageous persona. From her position of influence within the Mercure de France publishing house she had set herself up as the protector of avant-garde authors, especially those who were pushing against the boundaries of respectability and sexual norms. Oscar Wilde, Lord Alfred Douglas, Aubrey Beardsley and André Raffalovich were among her many correspondents and could all be sure of a warm welcome at the Mercure. Rachilde was immediately attracted to Jarry, it would seem, and

Rachilde in 1885.

Félix Vallotton, *Alfred Vallette*, woodcut, in Remy de Gourmont's *Le IIe Livre des masques* (Paris, 1898).

she is probably the only woman whose affection he unstintingly returned. Her masculinity appealed to him, as did her refusal to avoid shocking subjects. His letters to her are carefully crafted to earn her approval and he attended her Tuesday *salons* assiduously throughout his life.

Rachilde left a colourful biography of Jarry, *Alfred Jarry, ou le Surmâle des lettres*, echoing the title of his own novel, *Le Surmâle* or *The Supermale*. Her lively anecdotes about Jarry passed as a serious factual account of his life for many years. Unfortunately the time lapse of 21 years between his death and the publication of her book, together with her knack for telling a good story, led her to produce an over-dramatized version of Jarry's life. She omitted all the routine activities that he shared with them that would have given a more rounded portrait of the man. It is thanks to their daughter, Gabrielle, to whom Jarry first lent, then gave his Kodak camera, that a photographic record of Jarry and her parents at least exists.

Rachilde's account of Jarry's first appearance at her *salon*, portrays a brash young man who was not afraid of causing offence in new company. Another young writer was apparently holding a skein of silk for her while she stitched a tapestry. Rachilde claims that Jarry dashed it from the hands of this young man, protesting that it was a task for women. According to her account, she then tamed Jarry by binding the skein of silk around his hands instead. This was not the only time that she would reduce Jarry to a state of discomfiture, but her delight in playing tricks was to cost his career dear. Rachilde was later the instigator of a joke whose damage to her *protégé* she was unable to undo.

The year 1893 was one of success for Jarry in terms of creative output and establishing himself in literary circles, but also of personal loss. He shared the apartment rented by his mother at 84 boulevard de Port-Royal, but was renting a place of his own at no. 78, where he could sleep, receive friends and which he could decorate as he wished. Jarry nicknamed his tiny atelier the 'Calvaire du Trucidé', which roughly translates as 'Calvary of the Massacred Soldier.' Here he kept two owls, which some have recorded as live, and others stuffed. The walls were draped with black cloth, where a skeleton also hung, and the illumination consisted of a candle in a skull. However macabre his choice of décor, Jarry was at this moment materially comfortable.

In January Jarry caught a chill. Charlotte, the only witness to his illness, attributes their mother's subsequent death, a mere nine days after Alfred's recovery, to exhaustion from the forty-day vigil at her brother's bedside. 'Mama watches over him during forty days of winter, saves him and dies nine days later', she writes.[12] Her over-simplified version of events is questionable, disregarding as it does the passage of spring into early summer before Jarry's recovery.

Caroline Jarry, not yet fifty, died on 10 May 1893. A letter from Jarry four days earlier, excusing himself from an important banquet, describes her illness as serious attack of bronchitis and gives it as the reason that he cannot attend.[13] Charlotte's curt account contains more than a tinge of reproach, laying Caroline's death firmly at her brother's door. Jarry's notes from the spring term philosophy lectures of Henri Bergson, do not reveal any gaps, proving that the student could not have been bedridden for forty days, a period suspiciously equal to Christ's in the wilderness.[14] It is true, however, that, despite his admiration for his eminent philosophy teacher, and despite the fact that Bergson demanded that the students take every word of his lectures down, Jarry obtained the lowest mark in his class.[15] This may have been due to the shock of his mother's death rather than illness or absence earlier in the year. Their relationship had been close. Caroline's ambitions had been centred on her son. With her death, the importance of academic success might suddenly have faded. Portrayed by Jarry as 'a creature of a slightly different sex', and one of whom 'he had had to approve before he had a choice in the matter',[16] she had been a strong influence on him. The emotional impact of her death was considerable.

Death and love would thereafter be linked themes in Jarry's fictitious texts. His first book, *Les Minutes de Sable Mémorial*, which contains by far the majority of his whole poetic output, can be interpreted as a memorial to his early youth, the section of his life now ended by the death of his mother. The powerful closing poem of the collection, *Le Sablier*, in which a draining hourglass stands in for a bleeding heart, is one of lament, although the subject of the lament is not overtly named.

The role of Jarry's mother as a source of inspiration in his work is occluded but should not be overlooked. Keith Beaumont believed he never recovered from her death. He points to the 'grandiose memorial service' celebrated at the church of Saint-Jacques du Haut Pas in Paris on 11 May 1894, which, though paid for by his father, must have been at Jarry's initiative, so that his mother's memory would be honoured in the capital city itself and possibly at the church where she had worshipped.[17] Used as she was to the music of the massive organ at Saint-Brieuc Cathedral, its fellow at Saint-Jacques du Haut Pas would have naturally drawn her. The receipt for the cost of this service was found carefully preserved among Jarry's papers.[18]

Félix Vallotton, *Marcel Schwob*, woodcut, in Remy de Gourmont's *Le IIe Livre des masques* (Paris, 1898).

Whether or not written from his sickbed, the poems and prose pieces that Jarry produced during the first half of 1893 won five literary prizes between February and August of that year. Together with Fargue, he was a popular guest at the apartment of the erudite writer, Marcel Schwob (1867–1905), whose monthly *Écho de Paris* competition he had won with a triple contribution under the title *Guignol*. Part prose, part dramatic dialogue, *Guignol* represented Jarry's first attempt to launch the schoolboy comedy, *Les Polonais*, into the arena of adult literature. This experimental piece, *L'Autoclète*, in which Monsieur Ubu forces himself and his henchmen, the robotic Palotins, on the hospitality of the scientist Achras and then murders him, would be incorporated in the later *Ubu Cocu*. Ubu confounds his scientist host by introducing himself as 'a great pataphysician'. In the face of his bewilderment, Ubu simply announces that he has invented pataphysics, since it was a science whose lack was generally felt.[19] Jarry intended Ubu's remark to be funny. In this early piece the notion of pataphysics is unencumbered by the complex definitions that he later felt under pressure to provide.

Jules Flandrin, *Remy de Gourmont*, a pencil sketch of 1909.

Jarry dedicated *Ubu Roi* to Schwob. His visits and his readings from *Ubu Roi* did much to cheer the writer, suffering as he was with a form of syphilis that finally killed him in 1905. His companion, the actress Marguerite Moreno, relates how the announcement of certain visitors would cause his face to darken, but that Jarry's elegant conversation charmed him, and that his performance of *Ubu Roi* reduced him to helpless tears of laughter.[20] Schwob shared his literary enthusiasms with Jarry, who in turn relished hearing his friend read in English, whether from Richard Burton's translation of *The Thousand and One Nights*,[21] or the adventure stories of his friend Robert Louis Stevenson. Ill though he was, he undertook the long sea voyage to visit Stevenson in Samoa, arriving only after the writer's death. It was probably at Schwob's instigation that Jarry translated Stevenson's short story, *Olalla*.

The person whom Jarry made particular efforts to charm and to persuade of his literary talent, was, however, a very different character from either Rachilde or Schwob. Erudite bibliophile, critic and the descendant of a long line of master printers, Remy de Gourmont, a founder member of the Mercure de France, could make or break a new writer entering the literary mêlée. Jarry swiftly embraced Gourmont's various passions, whether for medieval woodcuts, Latin literature or old ballads. It was Gourmont who had discovered the manuscript of Le Comte de Lautréamont's *Les Chants de Maldoror* in the Bibliothèque Nationale, where he worked and published an article on them.[22] Jarry had no difficulty in absorbing Lautréamont's violent writing style and filled his play *Haldernablou* with Maldororisms. He dedicated the play to Gourmont, perhaps in the hope of appearing to be a successor to this strange poet.

Les Minutes de Sable Mémorial is an eclectic selection of pieces of very variable mood and quality. Jarry was writing in the final phase of the Symbolist era and his writing style of 1893–6 was marked by the hermeticism of that movement. His ideal and intended readership had had its responses sharpened by Mallarmé, whose well-known dictum was that to name an object in a poem removed three-quarters of its enjoyment. From the first Jarry set out to infuse his writing with maximum suggestive power and ambiguity. Words, for him, were not bound to a dictionary definition dictated by their orthography, but should be allowed multiple meanings.[23] Echoing Mallarmé, he wrote that it was important to 'Suggest instead of stating; create a crossroads where all words can come together in the great highway of sentences.'[24]

In his preface to *Les Minutes de Sable Mémorial* Jarry sets out his contract with his future readers, instructing them in the way they should approach all his future texts. It is an exhortation to use not only their eyes but also their ears in the business of interpreting the words that they read. He tells them to think of their ears as the pans of a jeweller's scales and to weigh words in them as carefully as if they were diamonds.[25] His preface is not a welcome to the reader but a warning.

(DILEMMA) By reason of the fact that one has written the work oneself, one has the advantage of active superiority over the passive listener. Every meaning that the reader will find has been foreseen, and he will never find all of them; the author can play Blind Man's Buff with his poor brain, suggesting unexpected, posterior and contradictory ones.[26]

In the face of this challenge Jarry's *Linteau* (Lintel), the title of his preface, does not seem a doorway through which the reader would step without misgivings. The author is standing like Cerberus in front of the door to his work, daring the reader to enter. Four difficult novels would follow *Les Minutes de Sable Mémorial.* It was not until Jarry began to write regular articles for *La Revue blanche* nearly a decade after the publication of his first book that he realized the benefits of writing concisely and clearly for the amusement of the general reader.

In the summer of 1893, however, following his mother's funeral and a rather bad performance in his exams, Jarry proceeded to fall out with his father over a trivial matter. He had returned to Laval for the holidays. Concerned to fulfil his parental duties and finding that his son had no overcoat for the autumn, Anselme took his son's measurements and ordered one from his tailor, choosing the cloth himself.[27] On delivery in October the cut of the coat was not to Jarry's taste and he sent it back to be taken in. It pleased him no better on its second appearance and he rejected it, insulting the tailor and returning to Paris without it. The injured tailor refused to take it back. When he added the 70-franc charge for the coat to Anselme's own bill, Anselme refused to pay. Both parties agreed to a court hearing, to which Jarry was summoned for 4 January 1894. It never took place. Suffering considerable loss of face in his hometown, Anselme was forced to report that his son had gone back to Paris the very morning of the hearing and to pay the full bill of 200 francs, plus costs. Substantial bureaucracy was involved, to which a seventeen-page legal document bears witness.[28] Although Jarry would have considered his father at fault for ordering a style of coat that he had not approved himself, his high-handed treatment of both the tailor and his father is an early presage of the way that he would handle debts in a less comfortable future.

The acrimony between father and son in the wake of this incident was never resolved. Jarry was on sick leave in Paris when Anselme died on 18 August 1895. He did not even make the effort of attending his funeral. Whether he was genuinely bed-bound with one of the viral infections that perpetually afflicted him, or whether he refused to attend is uncertain. Having been granted a temporary dispensation from his army service for ill health and facing possible hostility from his father's friends, he may not have wanted to show his face in Laval.

The death of Jarry's grandfather, Charles Quernest, had probably affected him much more deeply. From the age of six to fifteen in Saint-Brieuc his grandfather had been the main authority figure in his life. As he got older he had also had the run of his library. As Quernest's grandson, Jarry had more status in the town and at school than he had had as Anselme's son in Laval. On 4 February 1894 this learned gentleman, Justice of the Peace and author of various legal publications, followed his daughter to the grave. The impact of losing the two people who had overseen a particularly happy and secure period of Jarry's life should not be underestimated.

'Le Sablier' (The Hourglass), the well-named poem that closes *Les Minutes de Sable Mémorial*, refers obliquely to the landscape of sand and marshes that Jarry has left behind with his childhood. The adjacent illustration, which shows a schematic heart bleeding into the base of a broken bottle, connotative of drunken brawls, is an extraordinarily modern juxtaposition, stripping the theme of romance. Neither the poem nor the illustration gives any hint as to whether it is a particular person whose loss has caused the heart of the poet to be drained, and in whose memory the sand of his personal hourglass now spills out. Narcissistically, it spills into its own reflection, but the reflection lies on the surface of a marsh pool. The poem contains a suppressed anguish unmatched in the rest of Jarry's work and draws a line under the period of his childhood and adolescence.

Alfred Jarry, tailpiece woodcut of a heart bleeding into a broken bottle, from *Les Minutes de Sable Mémorial* (Paris, 1894).

3

The Art Magazine Editor

The month that Jarry spent with Paul Gauguin and the artists of Pont-Aven on Brittany's southern coast inspired him to try his hand at woodcuts. By mid-1894 he had probably already written and assembled most of the pieces that would make up *Les Minutes de Sable Mémorial*, but he had not finished the illustrations. The woodcuts for the volume would be engraved in Brittany during the summer. In a letter of 18 June 1894 Jarry wrote to Alfred Vallette, 'May I take the liberty of sending you the reduced block of an ugly little woodcut?'[1] This was the so-called *Weeping Heart* that would form the endpiece to *Les Minutes de Sable Mémorial*. Several of his other woodcuts for the book take their inspiration from the churches and cemeteries near Pont-Aven.

The painters of the so-called 'Groupe de Pont-Aven' represented some of the newest and most radical developments in French art. Pont-Aven's most famous visitor was Gauguin. 1894 was the year when Jarry began to break out of the mass of aspiring writers. He found that his Breton background, far from being a social disadvantage, could now be used to further his artistic career. As a part of their apprenticeships as writers, both he and Fargue were covering the avant-garde exhibitions, where many of the new Synthetist paintings emanating from Pont-Aven were being shown. Synthetism had evolved from the influence of Japanese prints, emulating their distinctive two-dimensional flat surfaces and bright colours. The Paris-based artist Louis Anquetin had been the first

Alfred Jarry, untitled woodcut with crosses and instruments of the Passion, adjacent to 'Le Miracle de Saint-Accroupi', from *Les Minutes de Sable Mémorial* (Paris, 1894).

to experiment with this style around 1887, together with Émile Bernard. Bernard had later worked in Pont-Aven with Gauguin and, according to him, introduced the older artist to the new technique. Gauguin had then returned to Tahiti and developed it in his own way, resulting in his sensational series of Tahitian paintings exhibited at the Galerie Durand-Ruel in November 1893.

Fargue had gone to Pont-Aven as early as September 1893 and made good use of his first-hand acquaintance with the painters in his reviews. Jarry might never had made this important visit had he not been summoned to the bedside of his mortally ill uncle in

Laval at the end of May 1894. Two weeks later, beset by boredom, while his uncle's condition neither improved nor worsened, Jarry decided to make the relatively short journey to Pont-Aven. He booked into the Pension Gloanec where Gauguin was bedridden with a badly broken leg. This had resulted from a fracas with fishermen at Concarneau, where Gauguin had invited his artist friends for an outing on 25 May. His conspicuous Tamil mistress, known as Annah, La Javanaise, had attracted a group of small boys, who were taunting her and throwing stones at the group. The artist Armand Seguin, who was walking with them, had grabbed one of the boys by the ear. The boy's father and his friends had then furiously set on him in turn.[2] While going to his friend's defence, Gauguin had fallen into a hole and broken his tibia so badly it protruded through the skin. The injury was slow to heal and he was immobilized for the summer. His lengthy convalescence condemned him to working indoors. Setting aside painting, he used the time to turn the subjects of his Tahitian paintings into woodcuts. As talented with a knife as with a brush, the artist now produced one of the most powerful series of woodcuts of the late nineteenth century.

Painters and local residents gathered outside the Pension Gloanec in Pont-Aven.

The little Pension Gloanec provided a home to a number of painters who were prepared to live very simply. The English artist Mortimer Menpes brought his wife and daughter Dorothy with him. Dorothy Menpes later described her mother's impression on arriving in the *salle à manger*, 'where rough men sat on either side of a long table, serving themselves out of a common dish, and dipping great slices of bread into their plates'. Her mother divided the painters into three categories: '*Stripists, Dottists* and *Spottists*, a sect of the *Dottists*, whose differentiation was too subtle to be understood'.[3]

Liberated from the claustrophobic atmosphere of his father's house, Jarry revelled in the stimulating company. He also had the opportunity to watch Gauguin at work. Some scholars have extrapolated from this coincidence that he learned the art of woodcutting from Gauguin. It is fairly certain that he was already adept at carving and easily turned this skill to woodcutting. In Pont-Aven he not only produced the woodcuts to illustrate his first book, but composed or completed poems on three of Gauguin's Tahitian paintings. Jarry carefully wrote the three poems in the Pension Gloanec's *Livre d'or*, dating them 1 July 1894 and dedicating them to Gauguin as a souvenir of his Durand-Ruel exhibition of November 1893. The *Livre d'or* was created by Gauguin and the three artists closest to him as a sacred record of their artistic brotherhood. The inscription that it carries begins as follows:

This day of 25 June 1894 We artists, being of noble race, born into the great and mysterious book of nature, Paul Gauguin, known as PGO, Eric Forbes Robertson, known as the Celt, Roderic O'Conor, Seguin the Jovial have decided
From this day on, this book, representing neutral ground between literary, painterly and musical art, will assemble the thoughts, drawings and signatures of all who will willingly join in our great work, eventually to meet again one day at the divine source of all forms.[4]

It seems that Jarry was admitted to the brotherhood and that his decision to commission the work of precisely these three painters for his and Gourmont's new magazine, *L'Ymagier*, was dictated by the bond between them. Jarry's homage to Gauguin was a very personal one. The paintings, *Manao Tupapau* (*The Spirit of the Dead Keeps Watch*) and *L'Homme à la hache* (*The Man with the Axe*), both commemorated important episodes narrated in *Noa Noa*, the narrative that Gauguin wrote to accompany his Tahitian paintings. Gauguin may well have suggested these paintings as potential subjects for poems.

Jarry's poems are often cited in catalogue commentaries for their sensitive interpretation of Gauguin's intentions, probably

Eric Forbes-Robertson, *Alfred Jarry*, portrait sketch, 1894.

acquired at first hand. His poem, *Ia Orana Maria* (*Hail Mary*) describes the winged angel of Gauguin's picture as 'a pallid bat from hell', reflecting the artist's negative attitude towards Christian teaching and the Catholic church. Gauguin's Tahitian Mary is attended by two native girls, whom Jarry calls the real angels in the composition. Clad only in loincloths, the girls represent a state of prelapsarian innocence, in contrast to the clothed Angel of the Annunciation, representing the Catholic priesthood, who is hiding furtively behind a bush.

Jarry's long article on Gauguin's friend, the reclusive artist Charles Filiger (1863–1928), written during or just after his stay in Pont-Aven, sympathizes with the interests of the group, whose art focused on the unsophisticated traditions and costume of the local people and the manifestations of their faith. The article is pitched to harmonize with the twin themes of religion and folklore which would feature in *L'Ymagier*. As well as Filiger himself, the article introduces the three Pont-Aven artists in the Brotherhood, the Irish painter Roderic O'Conor, Armand Seguin and Eric Forbes-Robertson, brother of the English actor Sir Johnston Forbes-Robertson and friend of Oscar Wilde. Jarry would also invite them to contribute to *L'Ymagier*.

The Filiger article is the most substantial piece of art criticism that Jarry wrote.[5] Over fifty years later André Breton would 'rediscover' Filiger, finally bringing his work to prominence on the strength of his faith in Jarry's judgement. Gourmont had previously commissioned Filiger to provide the frontispiece illustration to his book, *Le Latin mystique*. He may even have suggested that Jarry write the article. In fact he or his companion, Berthe de Courrière, may also have written a letter of introduction for him. It had actually been Courrière who had first introduced Gourmont to the artist.[6] Filiger was notoriously difficult to approach. When Fargue wrote to ask him to receive Jarry, he had refused to do so. This was

Charles Filiger in his studio, 1888.

admittedly in the wake of deceitful behaviour by Fargue, who had
borrowed some sketches during his visit and then attempted to
sell them to settle a debt.[7] Together with his undoubted charm
and enthusiasm, Jarry's new status as future co-editor of *L'Ymagier*
and his promise of paid commissions disarmed the artist, who
corresponded with him affectionately during the two years of the
magazine's existence.[8]

Filiger was regarded as a mystic. He had lived in Paris and
exhibited with the Salon du Rose+Croix, where Jarry would have
first encountered his work. He lived in a state of penury, depending
only on a small allowance granted to him by Count Antoine de la

Rochefoucauld, a Rose+Croix painter himself and editor of the magazine *Le Coeur*. He specialized in religious subject matter, adopting a medieval style that set him apart from the other painters of Pont-Aven. Under his brush, the local people who sat for him became transfigured into saints, their faces smoothed into expressions of extraordinary serenity. Gauguin and O'Conor, by contrast, tended to exaggerate the rough and evil cast of their subjects' features, especially when sketching the local boys. In her memoir Menpes did not recollect that the visitors held a high opinion of the locals: 'Many Bretons are scarcely of higher intelligence than the livestock of their farms. They live in the depths of the country with their animals, sleeping in the same room with them, rarely leaving their own few acres of ground.'[9] Émile Bernard, in his *Bretonneries* series of 1889, certainly made a point of accentuating the similarity between the Breton farmers and their animals. Jarry later described one of his paintings depicting peasants at market as no different from their fat yellow pigs, except that they wore blue, 'bursting out of their blue clothes like sausages out of their skins'.[10] Filiger refused to take this scornful attitude towards the peasants, preferring to depict poverty as an innocent if not sacred state.

Filiger's isolated life-style was not originally a matter of choice. He had been involved in a violent incident resulting from a homosexual liaison in Paris, after which he was found on the pavement, unconscious and bleeding profusely from a wound in his thigh and a severed artery in his hand.[11] He fled to Brittany in the wake of this incident, arriving there in July 1889. He quickly moved from Pont-Aven to the more isolated village of Le Pouldu, further east and right on the coast, where he could live more cheaply. He lodged at the tiny hostel run by Marie-Henry, known to her clients as Marie-Poupée. Gauguin had also taken refuge here with his friend Meyer de Haan, lured by the dramatic landscape of cliffs and sweeping sandy bay, well away from the increasing number of holiday painters at Pont-Aven. The happiest period of Filiger's life was probably the summer of 1890, spent working in the company of these two artists. When Jarry met him four years later, he had been living by himself for some time and was suspicious of intrusive visitors. Jarry saw him as a genuine mystic and was struck by the originality of his work. Filiger was one of the few painters close to Gauguin who had managed to maintain a powerful vision of his own. His homosexuality made him an *isolé* on two counts and a doubly deserving subject from Jarry's point of view. This was his first critical article and he had nothing to lose.

'Critic' was none the less a dirty word in range of Gauguin's hearing. It is noticeable that Jarry makes not a single allusion to Gauguin's work in the 'Filiger' article, while praising that of his other 'brothers in art', Seguin, Forbes-Robertson and O'Conor. It is likely that Gauguin had declined to contribute to *L'Ymagier* side by side with his one-time friend, and now rival, Émile Bernard, whom Jarry cites in an allusive parenthetical statement, placing his Synthetist style – his ability to simplify – on a par with Filiger's. The single wood engraving, *Madeleine*, credited to Gauguin that did appear in *L'Ymagier* was a copy by Seguin of a now lost monotype. Gauguin did not agree to contribute an original work. Moreover, the nude female figure huddled at the feet of the crucified Christ may have been an ironic reference to the devout Madeleine Bernard, Émile's sister, who had spurned Gauguin's advances.[12]

Jarry's article would have been difficult for him to write, torn as he was between the editorial commitment of *L'Ymagier* to the work of Bernard and his personal admiration for Gauguin. Possibly embarrassed by assuming the status of critic against his better judgement, he resolved his dilemma by performing an extra-ordinary about-turn in his final paragraph, denouncing art criticism as a valid procedure:

> It is quite absurd that I should be attempting to make a sort of *compte rendu* or description of these paintings. First of all, if they

were not very beautiful, I would have no pleasure in mentioning them and therefore would not do so.

Secondly, if I could explain point by point why they were very beautiful, that would no longer be anything to do with painting, but literature instead . . . and that would not be beautiful at all.

Thirdly, if I do not use comparisons to make my case – which would be quicker – it is because I do not want to do a disservice to those who may be leafing through these notes, by presuming that they need a shortcut to help them.[13]

Filiger was mistaken in identifying *L'Ymagier*'s young editor as a regular source of income and support. When Jarry broke with Gourmont after five issues of the magazine, he was unable to help the impoverished painter any further and their correspondence came to an abrupt close. Nor was Gourmont able to offer Filiger any commissions for the remaining three numbers of *L'Ymagier*. The magazine could not afford to operate as a charity.

Jarry would have found himself compromised in the bitter argument between Bernard and Gauguin, which hinged on who had been the master and who the disciple in developing the new style of painting. Bernard accused Gauguin of stealing his ideas and of using Christian themes without any religious conviction of his own.[14] Gauguin had built on Bernard's technical innovations but it was precisely his references to myths outside the Christian canon, together with his erotic, ironic and often personal allusions that gave his paintings their extra fascination over Bernard's. Jarry had enormous admiration for Gauguin and subscribed to his notion that only special individuals would understand the new forms of painting and writing that they were each pioneering. His poems pay tribute to Gauguin in the form that the painter would most appreciate. At the same time, he acknowledged Bernard as the pioneer and main representative of the pared down Synthetist style that he aspired to cultivate in his own writing. He would publish

Bernard's hand-coloured zincographs first in *L'Ymagier* and then in his own magazine, *Perhinderion*, linking his personal aesthetic principles to the artist's.

Jarry's and Gourmont's *L'Ymagier* project turned out to be one of the most significant contributions to nineteenth-century French illustration. The initial editorial statement emphasizes the magazine's commitment to popular imagery, especially coloured religious images from the Épinal factory. But it also commits to renovating imagery in general, promising to publish the work of the so-called new *imagiers*, citing Filiger and Bernard especially. The magazine lasted for eight issues, from October 1894 to December 1896, but Jarry was only involved in five issues before starting his own rival magazine. It is remarkable that he managed to combine military service with his editorship of those five issues. On the basis of his sister's notes, his biographers believe that he acquired dispensations or sick notes through the family doctor, a hunting friend of his father's, which enabled him to spend time in Paris. Charlotte writes:

> A year of military service in Laval. He eats in the officers' mess and his Corporal calls him 'Sir!' . . .
> Dr Dupré, Father's friend . . . frequent passes for him to go to Paris to start writing with the money that was supposed to be for the Sorbonne . . . One day, taken sick, he took part in the cycle race to Rennes: says the Commandant who hunted with his father: come on, old chap! You really are going to dump me in the sh**. Get out of here and go to Paris. At least we won't see you around![15]

Certainly Jarry made sure that he did not miss the famous cocktail party for 300 guests thrown during the harsh winter of 1895 by Edouard Vuillard's patron, Alexandre Natanson. This was a housewarming to show off the nine large decorative panels he had commissioned from Vuillard for the dining room of his new house at 60 Bois de Boulogne (now avenue Foch). Natanson had asked Henri de Toulouse-Lautrec to design the invitations and stage the party. Dressed in a white barman's suit with a waistcoat made out of the American flag, Lautrec put his imagination to work on the cocktails. The writer Paul Leclercq described pink cocktails to be sipped through a straw and throat-scorching cocktails of sardines in gin or port, which Lautrec set alight in a long silver dish. He was struck by the tiny form of Jarry sipping a ginger cocktail, alongside the tall thin critic, Félix Féneon.[16] Apparently they were among the first to succumb to Lautrec's lethal concoctions.[17] Allusions to Jarry before the première of *Ubu Roi* are rare and this is an interesting early record of his social progress beyond café society.

It is uncertain how much time Jarry spent in Paris during his military service. Only three letters from that period have come to light, far fewer than from other years and none was sent from Paris.[18] In one of these, unsure of the date of his release, Jarry asks Vallette not to send anything to his boulevard Saint-Germain address in case it goes astray. Instead, he recommends the address of *L'Ymagier*, 9 rue de Varenne, also home to Gourmont and Berthe de Courrière.[19] This suggests that he was confident that he would be able to pick packages up, even if his visits to Paris were sporadic. There is no known surviving correspondence between Jarry and Gourmont, which (though it may have been lost or destroyed) suggests that they saw each other so regularly that letters were superfluous. Jarry's frequent presence in this household may help to explain what happened later.

Jarry contributed an article to each of the five numbers of *L'Ymagier* in which he was involved. All but the first required specialist research. It is difficult to imagine that he could have accomplished this in the atmosphere of the military barracks in Laval. Nor would he have been able to execute the woodcuts that he published under the pseudonym Alain Jans. Gourmont had a hand press at home on which he could print his own woodcuts and those of his contributors. He left his apartment very rarely, as he was by now suffering from lupus, an autoimmune disease that disfigured his face. It follows that he had all the tools for making woodcuts to hand, which would also have been at Jarry's disposal. Jarry was indispensable to Gourmont for carrying out all the practical errands connected with running the journal, in terms of liaising with their printer, Charles Renaudie and the Épinal factory. This too would have been impossible to manage from Laval within the military routine.

In her biography of Jarry, Rachilde credits Courrière with arranging Jarry's discharge.[20] Although there is no evidence for this, he may well have avoided alienating her until clear of the army, in case she had the influence in senior military circles that she claimed. Jarry had been called up on 13 November 1894, one month after three significant literary achievements: he had published his first book, a major critical article, and brought out the first issue of the splendid, innovative *L'Ymagier*. He was discharged on 14 December 1895 and immediately broke with Gourmont.

With extraordinary speed he managed to bring out the first issue of his own larger format magazine, *Perhinderion*, in March 1896. It is difficult to believe that he could have designed and managed this ambitious publication so quickly without preparing the ground with Renaudie for some months. The folio format meant that the large Épinal images did not have to be folded in order to fit into the magazine, as with *L'Ymagier*. He rightly foresaw that *L'Ymagier*'s pullouts would eventually disintegrate across the lines of fold. Blind to expense, Jarry not only insisted on handmade paper, but had a special fifteenth-century typeface cast in order to make a faithful facsimile of Sebastian Münster's *Cosmography*, using the original Gothic lettering. Instead of publishing single pages as pictorial examples of early printing, as *L'Ymagier* had done, Jarry published entire chapters, so that the text could be read as a whole. Renaudie's press presided over the radical typographical innovations exemplified by Gourmont's books of the 1890s, which Jarry's took even further. He managed to fulfil the demanding printing and binding requirements of *L'Ymagier* and the even greater demands imposed by Jarry's ambitious design of *Perhinderion.* How many of these innovations were taken on his own initiative, we do not know. He must have been reassured that his clients had deep pockets, as the journals were custom-made to difficult specifications. Courrière's patronage had doubtless been crucial to the early numbers of *L'Ymagier.*

L'Ymagier represents an important landmark in the revival of the archaic woodcut in France. Jarry and Gourmont, both amateurs, are today perceived as two of the key innovators of this movement and forerunners of German Expressionism.[21] Their work is regarded by historians of the woodcut as more original than that of the several exhibiting artists who contributed to *L'Ymagier.* Jarry, however, seems to have seduced Gourmont into less honest practices than his judgement should have permitted. Both the editors published woodcuts under their own names, but for want of sufficient material they also published under the pseudonyms Richart Gheym and Alain Jans, names which corresponded to their own initials. Under his pseudonym, Jarry assumed the identity of a Flemish village artist, copying crude gingerbread moulds, manufactured to commemorate religious festivals. Gourmont was ultra-cautious in the use of his pseudonym of Gheym (similar to the German word for 'secret', *geheim*). Of the two woodcuts published under this name, one is in white ink so faint that its outlines can only be discerned in slanting light and the other was only available in the deluxe edition of the magazine. No other work under Gheym's signature is known.[22]

The editors set out their aims in the first number, stating that the magazine would contain nothing but pictures, from religious or legendary sources, and that the textual element would be very restricted.[23] But the commissioning of a lithograph of Henri Rousseau's striking painting, *La Guerre*, represented a completely new departure. Through this decision *L'Ymagier* stands out as a radical antecedent of the Munich-based *Blaue Reiter* almanac of 1912. The rudimentary grinning figure of *La Guerre*, holding a stick-like sword, and the squiggles representing the smoke from her torch, recall the efforts of children. It was the first time that anything similar had been considered worthy of publication in a magazine of such standing. The graphic style of *La Guerre* was already naïve in the extreme. It is hard to imagine Gourmont suggesting that this startling image be displayed on a pullout on a lurid orange ground, where it would dominate the entire magazine. The younger editor's intention to shock is unmistakable. The publication of Rousseau's *La Guerre* marked a distinct change in the direction and modernity of the magazine between the first and the second numbers.

The textual element of *L'Ymagier* was certainly much slighter than in the future *Blaue Reiter* almanac. The editors did not give advice about art or appreciating art, but for the second number of *L'Ymagier* Jarry wrote an important article, *Les Monstres*, illustrated with startling Cochin-Chinese woodcuts. It was here that he gave a highly original definition of beauty: 'It is customary to give the name *monster* to an unusual combination of dissonant elements: the Centaur and the Chimera being thus defined for those with no understanding. I give the name of *monster* to any original, inexhaustible beauty.'[24] Traditional views of beauty had already been challenged by Gauguin, who would later formulate his ideas in *Diverses choses*, writing that 'exquisite beauty cannot exist unless there is some strangeness in the proportions'. [25] Jarry's definition went further. When Breton discovered Jarry's article, he adopted his definition of beauty almost as a Surrealist credo.

Of all the contemporary artists published by *L'Ymagier*, Émile Bernard's work most represented the abstract, economical style that both editors favoured. He had been the first to experiment with the simple hieratic style typical of medieval woodcuts. Did Jarry know him personally? So far, there is no written record of this, but their coeval, the young director of the Théâtre d'Art, Paul Fort, whose productions they supported, would have drawn them together. In 1892 Fargue and Jarry helped Fort to found his magazine *Le Livre d'art*, with which Bernard was also closely involved, during what would be his last year in France until after Jarry's death.[26] Jarry's childhood home, Saint-Brieuc, was well known to him from the long walks that he took to the northern coast in summer, painting as he went. Jarry's admiration for the painter prompted him to write a chapter of homage to him in his novel *Faustroll*, designating the so-called *Bois d'Amour* in Pont-Aven as Bernard's personal artistic territory. In this chapter Jarry writes that Bernard gave Faustroll two large illustrated maps 'as a pure

Henri Rousseau, *La Guerre*, a lithograph published in *L'Ymagier*, no. 2 (1895).

Cochin-Chinese Warrior, a woodcut lent by Paul Fort, *Les Monstres*, *L'Ymagier*, no. 2 (1895)

gift'. He describes one as being like a tapestry representing groups of peasant women in their white coifs.[27] Is it possible that Bernard gave Jarry two pictures, even if these were not the ones described?

Jarry's relationship with Henri Rousseau (1844–1910), is much better documented than his relationship with Bernard. Rousseau, known as 'The Douanier' by virtue of his job as a collector of taxes, was Laval-born and had known Jarry's father since their school days. When Jarry got into difficulties Rousseau took a near parental role, twice stepping in to help his friend's son. On his side, Jarry used his authority as an art critic and magazine editor to promote Rousseau's work.

Rousseau was already well known to the self-styled 'Nabi' painters and respected by them. The word 'Nabi' means 'prophet' in Hebrew and was coined as a humorous title for themselves by the young artists studying together at the Lycée Condorcet, who, following Gauguin, had developed the new style of painting. These were Paul Sérusier, Maurice Denis, Pierre Bonnard, Édouard Vuillard and Ker-Xavier Roussel. A full three years before Jarry applauded Rousseau's exhibits at the Salon des Indépendants in 1894, the Swiss Nabi Félix Vallotton had sent an anonymous review of Rousseau's *Tigre surprenant une proie* to the *Gazette de Lausanne*, dubbing it 'the alpha and omega of painting' and marvelling at Rousseau's 'stupefying progress from year to year'.[28] Jarry, immersed as he was in the study of medieval woodcuts and Épinal images for *L'Ymagier*, possibly perceived analogies between Rousseau's childlike rendering of his subjects' faces and that of the self-taught religious engravers.

Shortly after the exhibition and perhaps in gratitude for Jarry's supportive reviews in both *L'Art littéraire* and *Essais d'art libre* Rousseau undertook Jarry's portrait. He had every faith in the future glory of the young writer from his own home town, whose first volume of poetry and prose pieces had just been published by the Mercure de France. There are conflicting accounts of this vanished work of art that created a stir at the eleventh Salon des Indépendants and which, according to a contemporary review, portrayed the writer surrounded by bats and owls. Louis Lormel, editor of the former *Art littéraire*, pointed out that one critic had mistaken the tongue of Jarry's pet chameleon for a pen-top stuck behind his ear. At the exhibition, the portrait was labelled as *Madame A.J.*, a mistake brought about by Jarry's shoulder-length hair at that time.

The portrait did not sell and Rousseau gave it to Jarry. Its eventual fate is unknown, and the accounts of those who saw it in Jarry's apartment some nine to eleven years later differ. Apollinaire claimed that only Jarry's head remained and that he had burnt away the background. When André Salmon visited Jarry's apartment in 1903 he reported that the mutilated background, consisting of some drapery with a hole in the middle, was still hanging there. Jarry said he had carefully cut his face out of the canvas and rolled it up in a drawer, explaining he was afraid that a visitor might attack and pierce his precious likeness with an umbrella.[29] It would seem that Jarry varied which part of the portrait he put on display.

At the time of Salmon's visit, Jarry had two china owls on his desk,[30] but ten years earlier he had been keeping live ones. This we know from a letter written by Jarry's landlord, reassuring him about the welfare of these difficult pets.[31] It was Rousseau, together with this obliging landlord, who, when Jarry was detained by his uncle's illness, offered to move all Jarry's things to his new lodgings in June 1894. Jarry had given notice for 1 July. Three years later, Jarry would be evicted from the same lodgings, but at this stage the absent young writer's credit was good and he was well liked – so much so that his landlord and a neighbour were prepared to lend a hand to help him out. On 26 June, five days after the death of Jarry's uncle, the long-suffering Rousseau, who was then also living in the boulevard Port Royal, wrote:

> Dear Sir
> I have been to fetch your palette and the box of famous actors, also the Japanese lantern which will look very passable in the trees; I started today, having expected you; and I shall work hard so that we can carry on as soon as you arrive. I have a message too from Mr. Donzé your landlord who has told me that he will take charge of your move if it is too much trouble for you to come down. Mr. Limony your downstairs neighbour will happily take it on with Mr. Donzé, if you could just let them know which day is best for you; they will even start straight away if you want . . . [32]

Rousseau's letter provides important evidence not only of Jarry's marionettes, including an earlier version of Ubu/Ébé than the surviving *Véritable Marionnette*, dated to 1897, but also of his activity as an amateur painter. At the end of his letter, Rousseau sends good wishes to Jarry's father, whose school career had briefly crossed with his own. The two Lavallois families knew each other well enough for them to witness each other's documents.[33] This information certainly undermines the apocryphal story that Jarry 'discovered' Rousseau. More to the point, the artist was determined to do his bit to help a friend of the family to fame. As a champion of novelty and with a nose for the potential of the naïve in art and literature, Jarry's support of Rousseau in return is not surprising.

With the history of friendship between the Rousseau family and the Jarrys, it is not surprising either that when Jarry was evicted from his lodgings in the summer of 1897, Rousseau should have offered his slight young friend a place in his bed. From his mention of Jarry's marionettes (the 'famous actors') he had obviously attended his puppet shows at his tiny apartment at 78 boulevard Port-Royal. This was located at the end of an alley so narrow that two people could not walk abreast. His assistants were Henri Morin and Léon-Paul Fargue, who, late in life, could still quote large chunks of *Ubu Roi* by heart. 'Le Calvaire du Trucidé' was more a miniature theatre space than a dwelling. Jarry had actually cut an aperture in one of his dividing walls, so that he could use it as a puppet booth. Blood red handprints marked the way up the ramshackle stairs to his door. In the gloom, his owls added to the spooky atmosphere. As long as the rent was coming in, his landlord was a tolerant man.

The happy relationship that Jarry had with his landlord and neighbours in 1894 was certainly due to his growing status as a published writer and to the appearance that he gave of having a private income. His move from the boulevard Port-Royal was to a much more prestigious apartment on the boulevard Saint-Germain. The money that he received from his father enabled him to buy shares in the *Mercure de France* and what may have been a substantial stake in *L'Ymagier*. One way or another, Anselme was certainly duped by his son.

With enough money in his pocket to write, and to frequent café society without having to work, 1894 was an extremely productive year for Jarry. In 1895 he faced military service, unavoidable to all males of his age group. He not only managed to juggle it with his literary career, but turned the experience into a novel.

4

Military Service: Fiction and Fact

Jarry's actual military service, of which there is little record apart from his novel, *Les Jours et les Nuits*, spanned the thirteen months between November 1894 and December 1895. He was due to be posted to Le Mans, but somehow strings were pulled to alter the posting to Laval, where the boredom and rigours of the barracks could be offset by invitations from friends of the family.[1] As late as 1947 a co-Lavallois called Gaston Roig, to whose section Jarry had been assigned, published his recollections from this period. To him we owe a portrait of Jarry, his shaven head balancing an overlarge red cap and swamped by his uniform jacket and trousers.[2] Roig related that he was sometimes included in the hospitality accorded to Jarry by his father's friends, which they were happy to repay with dramatic tall stories.[3]

The harshness of military life that Jarry paints in his novel was therefore mitigated by the very material advantages that were available to him in Laval. As a defence against the army routine, Jarry would have us believe that he set up a secondary existence inside his imagination, depicted as the 'desertion' of his alter-ego, the fictitious character, Sengle. The plot of *Les Jours et les Nuits* swings between the real experiences of the conscript and the idealized world of his childhood in the same landscape, filtered through memory.

The official note of Jarry's physical attributes on entry to the army, is useful in recording his exact height, if nothing else: '*Hair*: brown;

eyebrows: brown; *eyes:* brown; *forehead*: smooth; *nose*: medium; *mouth*: medium; *chin*: round; *face*: oval. *Height*: 1.61 m.'[4]

His lack of height gave him particular difficulty and made him a conspicuous figure of fun, as he struggled to overcome the shortness of his stride and keep up with the pace of the march. Roig gives a vivid account of Jarry's ridiculously stiff, robotic movements with his over-long rifle, as he endeavoured to perform the drills correctly. Jarry as Sengle complained that his arms were not long enough to hold the rifle in the regulation manner.[5]

Offsetting his comparative physical inferiority, Jarry made no secret of his literary status in Paris. This gave him some authority with aspiring soldier-writers. One of these appears in his novel under the name of Lieutenant Vensuet (*Vain souhait*) – a cruel reference to his vain literary aspirations – in reality a superior officer, Lieutenant Jean Tixier. Tixier gave Jarry some of his verse to read, hoping that he might give him an introduction to the *Mercure de France* (here renamed the *Iodure de Navarre*.) The verses that Jarry cites as Vensuet's are patently a parody of his own earlier style. They contain exaggeratedly erotic metaphor, some of which relates to his own unpublished poems of 1893–4. Sengle dismissively throws the poems ascribed to Vensuet into the fire, a gesture that has been interpreted as Jarry's renunciation of his own earlier 'Symbolist' work.[6]

Les Jours et les Nuits, roman d'un déserteur is structured in terms of the military reality of daytime, alternating with Sengle's 'desertion' into dream or reverie, chapter by chapter. Although published two years after his experience of soldiering, Jarry's account is probably the most biographically accurate of all his semi-biographical novels. He expresses his vivid distaste at the general issue uniform that still seems to carry within it the filth of previous wearers. Boots manufactured for the average male foot presented him with an even greater problem. The very smallest that he could find, even though he reinforced them with padding, still slipped and rubbed, forcing him to scrunch up his toes in order to keep them on, doubtless adding to the awkwardness of his marching gait.[7]

The rigours of the military drills are all the more poignant in Jarry's novel for the fact that they are performed in a landscape where he had roamed without restriction as a child. The passing scenery is full of familiar landmarks, each harbouring a specific memory or carrying a particular significance relevant to Sengle the child or teenage cyclist, but which the foot march embitters and annuls. He recognizes the bank where he used to chase crickets into their holes and block them up with his penknife; a rocky downhill track, that had once provided an exhilarating frame-shuddering ride on his bicycle, is entirely without excitement for the marching soldier. Sengle's attempts to absorb the passing land-scape and enjoy its associations, such as a pond where he used to watch the water beetles, are interrupted by whistle blasts and orders. A stream into which, as a child, he had once chased a snake, is now a freezing, hostile obstacle, impossible to jump in the encumbering uniform and with legs exhausted by the march. Sengle's memories, which Jarry inserts in the narrative by way of contrast to his pres-ent harsh experience, form an important series of snapshots of his own boyhood pastimes. They fill out Charlotte's brief allusion to her brother's fascination with insects as a child and his attraction to ponds.[8]

None of Jarry's other novels focus so strongly on landscape. Although by 1895 he had stopped commenting on art, the aesthetic creed of Gauguin and the Nabi painters can be discerned behind his observations of colours not usually associated with the things described: blue moss and reddish hedges, This creed had been passed to the Nabis by way of Paul Sérusier and his *Talisman* painting of 1888, produced according to Gauguin's advice: 'How do you see those trees? They're yellow. Well, use yellow; that bluish shadow, paint it with the purest ultramarine; those red leaves? Use vermilion.'[9]

Jarry would certainly have read Gauguin's article 'Natures mortes', his tribute to Vincent van Gogh. It had appeared in the January 1894 number of *Essais d'art libre* just before Jarry's own first article was published there. Gauguin had recalled van Gogh's love of the colour yellow, describing the painting of sunflowers that hung in his own room and the brilliant effect that the sun shining through his yellow curtains had on the painted blooms.[10] In *Les Jours et les Nuits* Jarry adopts yellow as the colour of happiness. One of the chapters, 'Consul Romanus', in which Jarry seems to integrate his own memories of Pont-Aven with its characteristic yellow broom flowers, is particularly suggestive of Gauguin. Here yellow is the dominant backcloth to a romantic bathing scene between Sengle and his friend, Valens.[11] Valens is described in terms of a golden statuette, much the same image as Jarry had used of the man in his poem, *L'Homme à la Hache*, based on Gauguin's painting. In *Noa Noa* Gauguin had implied that his painting commemorated a moment of erotic attraction that he had felt for a handsome young woodcutter.[12] Through his poem and through this chapter too, Jarry was hoping to link Gauguin's imaginative universe with his own. *L'Homme à la hache* was, however, a very rare example of a male subject in Gauguin's work, and he may not have appreciated Jarry's publishing his poem of homage in a book devoted to male love.

Whether or not Jarry's vivid description of the bathing boys, a popular subject with Pont-Aven painters, related to a real experience, the chapter represents Sengle's escape into reminiscence. He was 'deserting' from the very different bathing experience of compulsory showers described in the previous chapter. There, although sick, he describes how he was forced with the others to strip down to his shirt and wait in the freezing cold, queuing until the previous companies had finished. Jarry's health was never robust and his exemptions for sickness were probably valid, even if he abused them by entering for local cycle races as recorded by Charlotte, or by sneaking into town for a proper bath, as Sengle does. Sengle's fastidiousness, related to his middle class upbringing, no doubt reflects Jarry's own. He is revolted by the mud that sticks to his gun and clothes and the filthy slime that accumulates in the communal showers. He also misses the privacy that would allow him to read.

From a biographical point of view *Les Jours et les Nuits* is important for its allusions to an emotional attachment immediately before Sengle's conscription. Jarry explains the title of the book as referring to the fact that, for Sengle it was not the moon or the sun that marked his nights and days but the shining presence of his friend.[13] In the section of the novel titled 'Le Livre de mon frère', Sengle recalls an experience with this friend that had deeply affected him. Having offered this information, he back-pedals, pretending that he is no longer sure whether the friend had really existed, finally insisting that in fact he had not, and that Sengle was narcissistically in love with a younger version of himself. This would seem to be a subterfuge, as he had earlier said that Valens had left France and was 'vegetating in disease-ridden India'.[14]

Sengle complains that the sixty-day period needed for a letter to travel to India meant that the writer had to wait four months to get a reply. The remark has a ring of irritation that seems to reflect the author's own experience. At another stage in the novel he mentions that Valens was going to be away for ten months. What would be the point of these fretful and precise details if not real? The poem that commemorates this friendship is extraordinary in Jarry's oeuvre for the tender note that it strikes, so out of tune with the recently published *Ubu Roi*, with which his name was by now indelibly associated:

I don't know if my brother remembers me at all,
But now I feel alone, enormously alone,
His dear, distant face paling in my efforts
To retrieve a lying memory.

I have his portrait before me on the desk.
Was he handsome or not? – I don't know.
This Double is useless and hollow as a tomb
For I have lost his voice, his adorable voice.

Its true note now seems falsified on purpose.
A posthumous treasure that he knows nothing of.
Beyond what writing can express I suddenly can sense
Its broken and feathery caress.[15]

Despite his apparent attempts to throw the reader off the trail, Jarry lays some clues that have enabled future researchers to discover the identity of Valens. Sengle refers to a book on heraldry where he claims to have found his and the Valens' family arms a few pages apart. This has now been identified as J.-B. Rietstap's *Armorial général*.[16] From the descriptions of the arms given by

François Benoît
Claudius-Jacquet,
from a group
photograph taken
at Lycée Henri IV.

Jarry it was possible to pinpoint Sengle's arms as those of the Jarry family from Maine, and Valens' arms as those of the Jacquet family of Lyons. This leads us to François-Benoît Claudius-Jacquet, a younger boy at the Lycée Henri IV, the shadowy figure who Patrick Besnier believes to be the great love of Jarry's life.[17] He will appear again in his correspondence.

Apart from the swimming scene, which may be an artificial construct, there are two other shared experiences with Valens / Claudius-Jacquet that seem to have deeply affected Jarry as Sengle. The first was a highly charged walk in the woods, where Sengle describes being in a state of elation as if he had taken hashish. Through his description of Sengle's feelings, Jarry's own fear of physical contact is transparent. Sengle is so anxious that the charmed atmosphere between Valens and himself might be broken by an over-intimate gesture that he instructs Valens not to touch him. He invents a complicated story about his astral body and his soul floating above them, attached by a visible thread as if to two kites. Citing a Chinese legend, his unlikely theory is that the thread will break if he is touched, causing him to die.[18] It would seem that Jarry as Sengle was fearful of the relationship moving on to another, more dangerous level, beyond the realm of boyish pleasures. The sentimental tone of these passages could not have been more different from that of *Ubu Roi*. Linked as it was to the name of the scandalous and funny Alfred Jarry, the publication of *Les Jours et les Nuits* in July 1897 disappointed expectations. The novel fell flat.

Contrary to the sentiments expressed in his novel, Jarry had actually conformed perfectly well to army discipline and earned a commendation for good conduct when he was discharged. It has never been clear how his early discharge came about. It came into effect on 14 December 1895, a full two years ahead of the normal term. The reason given was 'chronic biliary lithiasis', which, in lay terms, refers to stony concretions forming in the bile duct. In *Les*

Alfred Jarry, 'Je te dis *merdre, merdre, merdre, comme cette sale Mère Ubu*',
ink sketch, 1895.

Jours et les Nuits Jarry describes various ruses to simulate illness
suggested to him by his friend Maurice Dide, who appears in the
novel as the character Nosocome. Certainly very ill and with a high
fever, Jarry was admitted to the Val-de-Grâce Hospital in Paris, where
he occupied the bed next to Max Lebaudy, heir to the Lebaudy
sugar fortune and witnessed the brutal procedures to which he was
subjected, with fatal consequences.[19] Noël Arnaud believed that
Jarry must have been discharged on the basis of a genuine medical
condition.[20] Yet Roig's chance meeting with Jarry left him with the
impression that, as recounted by Rachilde, there had been a high
level intervention on his friend's behalf.[21]

On 15 December, the very day after his discharge, Jarry was
certainly in high spirits and reasonably good health. This is apparent
from his rumbustious note to an unknown recipient, addressed
only as 'mon cher ami'. He was well enough to be taking the train to
a lunchtime rendezvous in Chatou and fitting in a meeting with his
friend beforehand. To this warm note Jarry added the only known
drawings of Mère Ubu by his hand. 'I say *merdre, merdre, merdre*, to

you like this filthy Mère Ubu', he wrote, adding a steaming pile of excrement to his sketch.[22]

In 1895, at the same time as his military service, Jarry was writing his densely Symbolist drama *César-Antechrist* and shouldering his share of the editorial responsibility for *L'Ymagier*. His professional relationship with Gourmont meant that he could not avoid spending time at his home at 9 rue de Varenne and coming into contact with his companion, the predatory Berthe de Courrière. She had had a chequered sexual history. At the age of twenty she had first become the mistress of General Boulanger and after that of several ministers. A large, curvaceous woman, she had been Jean-Baptiste Auguste Clésinger's model for the bust of Marianne, national emblem of the French Republic, and for the colossal statue of the Republic that he sculpted for the Universal Exhibition of 1878. He made her his heir and she inherited his considerable fortune when he died in 1883. In 1886 she met Gourmont and commissioned him to write a monograph on Clésinger. She became his mistress, his muse and the heroine of his novels *Sixtine* and *Fantôme*. His passionate letters to her were later published as *Lettres à Sixtine*.

Gourmont was a founder member of the *Mercure de France*. Courrière was thus a regular visitor to Rachilde's *mardis* and became the butt of many jokes. According to Rachilde, whose 1928 account is highly coloured, the writer Jean de Tinan was particularly irritated by her. Placing the blame largely on Tinan, she writes that they concocted an amusing plot to get rid of both Courrière and Jarry, 'the two monsters encumbering my salon, in Tinan's view'.[23] Rachilde's account indicates that the plot may have been unleashed in September 1894, following Jarry's return to Paris after his trip to Pont-Aven, for she places Courrière's intercession in the matter of Jarry's discharge as being after her failed attempts to seduce him. Jean-Paul Goujon, Tinan's biographer, dates the affair to the period between the autumn of 1895 and the beginning of 1896, which seems more probable. He suspects Rachilde of shifting the blame on to Tinan who was dead by the time of her memoir. He finds no evidence of Tinan's ill will towards Jarry. 'Jarry's imagination has overtaken us all', Tinan had said.[24]

Rachilde relates that she discreetly mentioned to 'our *Vieille Dame*', that Jarry often took on a dreamy look when she was talking and that he had praised her singing voice.[25] She gave Courrière the notion that she, of all people, 21 years his senior and nicknamed 'Berthe Big-Feet', might have the chance of diverting Jarry from his attraction to the male sex. Incredulous at first, Courrière's interest in Jarry was apparently aroused.[26] Rachilde fails to point out that Jarry was forced, on his return, to spend a lot of time at 9 rue de Varenne, liaising with Gourmont on the launch of *L'Ymagier*, to which the funds provided by Courrière were crucial. As well as the instructions for the printer, the name 'Berthe' is tellingly scrawled at the top of his 'Filiger' article in blue crayon, not in Jarry's hand, but Gourmont's. Jarry's appointment as joint editor with Gourmont was dependent on her approval as well as the critic's. Knowing that Courrière held the purse strings he probably exerted his charm on her as much as on Gourmont. Rachilde enjoyed her power as wife of one of the most influential editors in Paris. It is likely she resented the fact that another woman might be in a position to influence the career of this difficult young writer, whom she prided herself on taming. If so, her machinations certainly succeeded in creating an irreparable rift between Jarry and his two main patrons, isolating him and making his success or failure more dependent on her influence.

Reputedly a nymphomaniac, Courrière was vulnerable to Rachilde's cruel trick. Moreover, by making it embarrassing for Jarry to go to 9 rue de Varenne, his collaboration on *L'Ymagier* with Gourmont was undermined, endangering the careful foundations he was laying towards establishing his reputation. Courrière began to send Jarry messages inviting him to meet her. First there was a note enclosed in the pages of a book she sent him, that he failed even to open; then, more pressingly, telegrams. Rachilde's biography retails Jarry's pungent comments about Courrière's onslaught. At the same time Rachilde projects the image of herself as the only woman that he was prepared to count as his friend.

Whatever the truth of Rachilde's account, Jarry obviously succeeded in managing his relationship with the Gourmont household for the sixteen months that he co-edited *L'Ymagier*. His own, admittedly fictitious, account of Courrière's advances is given in his later book, *L'Amour en Visites*. In the unsparing chapter, 'La Vieille Dame', he published every one of Courrière's cloying missives. Here she is speaking in Jarry's merciless portrayal:

> I've changed my dress in front of you five times, and you haven't looked. I have dresses split up the side, so that my yellow pants can be seen underneath, and only a single hook needs to be undone for the whole dress to slide off. And I had them made especially for affaires.
>
> I never wash except with Vaseline. I buy it on the cheap from a back-street chemist, who also supplies me with anti-herpetic ointment.
>
> That's how I've kept my skin in such good condition. Oh! Don't look at me in the light like that. Those are only little red spots.[27]

Rachilde did remonstrate with Jarry for attacking Courrière, a person who was unbalanced and not responsible for her actions, in her view.[28] She was worried that serious repercussions would ensue. For him the vicious chapter seems to have been a way of cleansing himself and of distancing himself from an association that he had borne with difficulty.

The newly inherited money resulting from his parents' death had made Jarry reckless. Gourmont's support had served its initial purpose of launching him as a writer. With his rebuff and ridicule of Courrière he jettisoned it, sacrificing not only his place as a Mercure de France author, but a potential place in Gourmont's later *Livre des masques*, his important gallery of contemporary writers. Neither Jarry nor Rachilde can have appreciated the grave repercussions that the injury to Gourmont would have on Jarry's future wellbeing. In 1894 and 1895 Jarry had seemed on the path of a promising literary career. Exactly how it was going to develop was impossible to predict. He and his friends had no inkling that his fame would flare explosively and briefly in 1896, in an event that would make theatrical history, but which masked the fact that the seeds for his personal downfall had already been sown.

At the end of 1895 Jarry blithely embarked on his rival publication to *L'Ymagier*, his expensive folio journal *Perhinderion*. Through *Perhinderion*, the Breton word for *Pardon* in the sense of 'pilgrimage', Jarry wanted to evoke the religious pilgrimages of his childhood and assert his identity as a Breton. The journal would only survive for two issues, published in January and June 1896. In deciding to have a fifteenth-century typeface cast especially for the journal Jarry had probably not taken the potential cost into account. The typeface was a whim that Vallette, writing Jarry's obituary, highlighted as one of his typical childish impulses, followed through without any regard to consequences.[29] Quite apart from following the unorthodox spelling of Sebastian Münster's text, setting the original fifteenth-century Mazarin fonts, found by Renaudie, in which the difference between the *s* and the *f* was almost indistinguishable, must have been a compositor's nightmare.

Jarry admitted that the result was imperfect and announced that the typeface was to be cast anew for the second and subsequent numbers.[30] Broke and unable to continue beyond the second number, he lent the typeface to Paul Fort for *Le Livre d'art*. Fort also used it to print his edition of *Ubu Roi*, published in July, ahead of the as yet uncertain Théâtre de l'Œuvre production. Jarry's insistence on the highest quality handmade paper and a

Comment beftes venoyent de tous coftez

& de loing, audit eftang.

Pres qu'Alexâdre le grâd eut campé & affiz font fort pres de ceft'eftâg, ainfi que les fouldardz cômençoyent à dormir leur premier fomne, et que la lune iettoit fes premiers rayôs : voicy incontinêt vne trouppe de fcorpions ayâs les aiguillôs de la queue dreffez, qui felon leur couftume venoyêt la pour boire, & fe fourrerêt parmy le câp en fort grâd nôbre. Apres les fcorpions, on vit venir vne autre bâde de ferpês nommez certaftes, & d'autres ferpês de diuerfes couleurs. Car aucûs auoyêt les efcailles rouges : les autres eftoyêt côme iaunes, & les autres noirs & blâcs. Tout le pays retêtiffoit de fifflemês, & n'y auoit fi hardy Macedonien qui n'eut peur. Toutesfois pour refifter contre telz ennemys, ilz auoyêt mis au deuât de tout leur oft vn grâd nombre de paucis : & renoyent en leurs mains des halebardes, piques & autre long bois, defquelz ilz tuerent beaucoup de ces mauuaifes beftes, & en feirent mourir plufieurs par feu. Cela les tint en grand foucy l'efpace de deux groffes heures. Or apres que ce beftial ferpentin eut beu, les petizs' en retournerent, & les plus grand les fuyuirent : qui donna grande ioye à tout le camp. Apres cela enuiron les trois heures apres minuict, ainfi que les Macedoniês s'attendoyent de recouurer quelque repos, fe prefenterêt des ferpens ayans creftes ou coronnes fur la tefte : les vns auoyêt deux teftes, les autres trois, au demeurant vn peu plus gros que pilliers ou pofteaux : lefquelz eftoyent fortiz des cauernes voifines pour venir boire faifans grand bruyt de leurs gueules & efcail les. Ilz faifoyent fortir hors leurs langues à trois pointes : ilz auoyent les yeux eftincelans de force de venir & leur haleine eftoit infecte & dangereufe. Les Macedoniens les côbatirent vne heure ou plus : & en ce combat furêt occiz vîgt hô mes de guerre

& trente feruiteurs. Apres qu'ilz furent deliurezde ces ferpens, voicy vn nombre infiny de tâcres ou efcreuices couuertz de peaux de crocodiles, qui vinrent au camp. Ces beftes a

custom-made typeface incurred expenses that his modest inheritance could not cover. He honoured his bill of 259.85 francs for the Mazarin typeface to Renaudie, who eventually bought it back. With the realization that a third number of *Perhinderion* was beyond his pocket, Jarry was forced to change direction. Fortunately he had been preparing a parallel career.

5

'After Us the Savage God'

Two stage performances of *Ubu Roi* were put on by the Théâtre de l'Œuvre on 9 and 10 December 1896 respectively. They brought the name of Alfred Jarry to national prominence and catapulted Ubu, the ridiculous puppet character that he had adopted and fostered, to the status of one of the great comic prototypes. During the four years of his Paris existence before 1896, Jarry had been one young writer among many. He certainly had a leading role in avant-garde book design, but the two limited edition books that he had published in 1894 and 1895, *Les Minutes de Sable Mémorial* and *César-Antechrist*, were not accessible to the general reader and were not even easy for his writer acquaintances and friends to follow.

Non-conformist as he was in his basic temperament Jarry had followed Symbolist literary practice, but pushed Symbolist obscurity and ambiguity to its limits. Meanwhile the caricature figure of Ebé/Ubu, for whom Jarry's victim Monsieur Hébert had been the model, had lodged itself in his psyche. Ubu had become an inerad-icable, lurking presence in his imaginative landscape. The punchy, vulgar dialogue of the puppet play, composed by clever teenagers, fitted perfectly into the café culture of the late 1890s, fostered by the Chat Noir cabaret. Jarry's delivery of the Ubu dialogue in his 'special voice' reduced his literary friends to helpless laughter. It is no wonder that he wanted to test the potential of the Ubu playlets as literary texts.

Jarry's first assay had been to include an Ubu fragment, pompously titled *L'Autoclète* (*The Uninvited Guest*), with two other prose pieces, under the overall heading of *Guignol. Guignol* won the monthly prose prize of the *Écho de Paris* competition of April 1893 and he decided to include it in *Les Minutes de Sable Mémorial*, alongside his Symbolist poems and prose poems. His next step was to put together a much larger dramatic piece from the Hébertique cycle. It was a condensed version of the eventual text of *Ubu Roi* and included it as a single act within his obscure play, *César-Antechrist*. Jarry's intention was to lift the character, Ubu out of its comic context, presenting him as a destructive counterpart to the Antichrist. He wanted to put the play not only in a Symbolist but an occultist framework, in order to give the frivolous schoolboy product solid intellectual credentials.[1]

The elements that finally brought this improbable play to the Paris stage were extremely unpromising. Jarry had failed in his own publishing venture, he had lost his influential patron, and the Mercure de France publishing house would no longer issue his work. Rachilde, Paul Fort and Marcel Schwob rallied to help the now impoverished writer. Jarry's performances with his puppets at the Mercure de France offices had caused such mirth that Rachilde, in particular, decided that the play had wider potential and made up her mind to use her influence with Aurélien Lugné-Poe, director of the Théâtre de l'Œuvre, to get it produced. In 1893 Lugné-Poe had followed up on Paul Fort's ambitious but ephemeral Théâtre d'Art project, founded in reaction against realist 'slice of life' theatre. Art and literature had long since reacted against naturalism. Now Lugné-Poe's Théâtre de l'Œuvre finally responded to calls for a Symbolist theatre.[2] It was Fort who took it upon himself to publish the full text of Jarry's would-be play to enable its production. French playwrights had so far been poorly represented in the Œuvre's programme by comparison with Scandinavians. Jarry's play would help to redress the balance.

Alfred Jarry,
Véritable portrait de Monsieur Ubu, 1896,
woodcut.

Fort claimed that, with the help of the artists Charles Guérin and Eugène Paul Ullman, he had had to tear the pages of the manuscript out of the enraged Jarry's hands in a physical fight, which cost them several handfuls of hair. It was they, wrote Fort, who put the scenes in their eventual order during a single night. Jarry had apparently admitted that the text was in disarray and that he wanted to burn it.[3] This claim was not verified by Jarry, who, while never asserting sole authorship over *Ubu Roi*, insisted that he himself had established the final order of the scenes. He had also conceived a new haunting visual representation of Ubu, an occult spiral incised on his huge belly and a pointed hood or mask, that recalled the costume of the Spanish inquisitors. This was the illustration that appeared on the cover of the *Livre d'art* edition of *Ubu Roi*.

Whatever misgivings Jarry might have had about the potential success of *Ubu Roi* on the stage, it is not apparent from his letters to Lugné-Poe. They are among the most detailed in his surviving correspondence and form a part of theatre history in themselves. At first he had established his literary credentials with the director by sending him copies of *L'Ymagier*. At the practical level, it is probable that he also took bit parts in some of the productions under a pseudonym.[4] When the post of administrator for L'Œuvre fell vacant in June 1896, Jarry hastened to offer his services. Judging from a subsequent letter of Rachilde's to Lugné-Poe, it would seem that he offered them gratis. Lugné-Poe was delighted to have such an energetic assistant who cycled hither and thither, collecting subscriptions, even from the most recalcitrant, and getting rid of importunate creditors.[5] In addition Jarry's experience in printing was extremely valuable when it came to the theatre programmes. He presided over some of the most innovative theatre programme illustration of the era by Édouard Vuillard, Edvard Munch, Félix Vallotton, Pierre Bonnard and himself. The brightly coloured publicity poster for *Ubu Roi* may well have been printed on his own press at 162 boulevard Saint-Germain. A letter inviting the artist Maurice Delcourt to bring him any colour woodcuts he needed to pull makes it clear that he had set up his own printing and binding facilities and, unusually for this date, had the facilities to print in colour.[6]

In his memoirs, with the benefit of hindsight, Lugné-Poe traces what he later recognized to be a cunning softening up campaign designed by Jarry to persuade him to undertake the production of *Ubu Roi*. He knew that Jarry had a play in mind, but had no idea what kind. In his letters to Lugné-Poe, Jarry treads a cautious path.

In January 1896 he had submitted *Les Polyèdres*, a version of the future *Ubu Cocu*, for his consideration. In March 1896 he retracts it with the excuse that a part had already been published (*L'Autoclète*) and that it had been written in haste. At the same time he begs mysteriously to be allowed to submit 'something that may be sent to me of which I am very fond', at some future date. Before the beginning of the year he had already shown a version of *Ubu Roi* to Lugné-Poe, but the director had been unable to work out a way of staging it. In January he boldly sets out his ideas in a letter, ideas that he had calculated would chime with Lugné-Poe's own views, but which would also be crucial for theatre history:

1. A mask for the main character, Ubu, that I could procure for you if necessary . . .
2. A cardboard horse head that he would hang round his neck, as in the Old English theatre . . .
3. Adoption of a single set, or better still a plain backdrop, avoiding having to put the curtain up and down during the one act. As in puppet plays, a well-dressed character would come in and hang up a notice saying where the action was taking place. (Note that I am certain of the 'suggestive' superiority of a written sign over a painted backdrop. Neither a backdrop nor the use of extras could convey 'The Polish Army Marching Through the Ukraine.')
4. Avoid crowd scenes. They often misfire on the stage and make it difficult to know what is going on. Thus, just a single soldier in the scene of the review and another in the *mêlée*, where Ubu says 'what a crush of people, what a stampede etc.'
5. Adoption of a special 'accent' or even better special 'voice' for the main character.
6. Costumes as little related to local colour or historical time as possible (giving a better impression of something eternal),

preferably modern, since satire is modern; and sordid, because the play will appear all the more wretched and horrific.[7]

L'Œuvre was run on a shoestring and Jarry was careful to assure Lugné-Poe that his suggestions would involve no cost, which turned out to be far from the truth.

For the time being *Ubu Roi* was put on ice. Jarry threw himself into managing other productions. Ibsen's large cast production, *Peer Gynt*, which opened on 12 November 1896, was a particular challenge. The Moulin Rouge dancer Jane Avril was persuaded to take the part of Anitra. Munch's playbill gives Kobold, a professional clown, as Old Man of the Dovrë and Jarry as First Troll of the Court. Lugné-Poe was grateful for Jarry's comic talents when it came to interpreting the troll scene, whose particular humour he had worried would not appeal to a French audience.[8] Jarry also took on the task of editing the play into a more succinct, produceable form. Although damaged by a binder's over-zealous guillotine, his pencilled additions, which replace the cuts to the printed text, still partially survive on the acting proofs.[9]

Jarry's hard work and success with this production must have given Lugné-Poe confidence in his abilities, for he now agreed to follow *Peer Gynt* with *Ubu Roi*. Unfortunately Jarry's intransigent and apparently excessive demands about the way he wanted the play performed made him think again. It then took a stern letter from Rachilde to press him to keep his word to the young author and prove his eclecticism. With the authority of her *mardi* salons at the Mercure de France, she claimed that the entire younger generation was waiting for him to put on *Ubu*. She further offered a suggestion completely at odds with Jarry's idea of stage practicality, that the puppet-like character of the actors should be emphasized by attaching them to strings leading from the wings. She also warned against an introductory speech – sensibly as it turned out.

She finally suggested that her husband might intercede with Jarry to persuade him to make some compromises.[10]

What were Jarry's demands, which Lugné-Poe found so exasperating? The director describes him as 'a sort of tormented genius, who caused a thousand ever thornier difficulties to spring up under our feet'. His helpful assistant had suddenly turned into a monster. The insouciant extravagance evident in his free-handed doling out of commissions for *L'Ymagier* and the perfectionism that had beggared him with *Perhinderion* now endangered Lugné-Poe. The director arrived one morning to encounter a lifesize horse and forty as yet unclothed, lifesize wicker mannequins, destined to represent the nobles and bourgeois whom Ubu would cast down the hatch. It was an idea of genius, but wholly unaffordable. Jarry's assurance that the vendor would take them back after the performance did not turn out to be correct. Lugné-Poe not only had to pay for them and find costumes for them, but was stuck with storing them afterwards. Casting live actors down the hatch would not have represented the slapstick, *guignolesque* humour that Jarry wanted. The visionary, modern solution of mixing inanimate mannequins with live actors was the ideal that he came up with for adapting the violent puppet play to the full-size stage. It would be over twenty years in 1917 before a similar concept could be put into practice, on a Ballets Russes budget, in the form of Jean Cocteau's *Parade* with stiff body masks designed by Picasso and music by Eric Satie, whose instrumentation, against the composer's wishes, included milk bottles and a foghorn. Even so, to bring this production about needed the intervention of Misia Edwards, who, as the former Misia Natanson, wife of Thadée Natanson, editor of *La Revue blanche*, had known Jarry well and attended the *Ubu Roi* dress rehearsal.

For *Ubu Roi*, Jarry asked that the live actors make their movements stiff and jerky in the manner of wooden marionettes, and we know from W. B. Yeats's account of the performance that this was actually put into practice.[11] Jarry had not initially envisaged a musical accompaniment, but when the avant-garde composer Claude Terrasse learned through his brother-in-law, Pierre Bonnard, that Lugné-Poe was putting on the play, he got in touch with Jarry to offer to compose one. Although Terrasse then composed a special piece for a variety of fairground instruments, the accompaniment finally had to be restricted to the piano, which he played himself, and the drum. Jarry was mortified that the instruments could not be assembled, and said so in his introductory speech: 'It was very important that, in order to be serious about being marionettes, we should have had fairground music. We have not had time to get together the brass, gongs and trumpets marine, between which the orchestration should have been divided.'[12]

It was not only Lugné-Poe who had his doubts about the play. Firmin Gémier, the actor chosen to play the part of Ubu, could not perceive how he was going to interpret the role. Furthermore, he was worried that by taking the lead in this scandalous play he would jeopardize his permanent position at the Odéon. Lugné-Poe advised him to imitate Jarry's own staccato voice on only two notes, reproducing the delivery of Ubu's prototype, Monsieur Hébert. This technique turned out to be the most successful, although Gémier complained that the heavy triangular cardboard mask that encased his head made it almost impossible for him to breathe, let alone speak. When he reprised the role after Jarry's death he refused to wear a mask at all. The transformation of human actors into puppets certainly had its problems. A sharp letter from Jarry to Lugné-Poe dated 6 December 1896 insists that unless the director can hold the play back for a week in order to give Gémier time to get into the role, it should be dropped entirely. The writer was not one to make compromises.[13]

Jarry had taken pains to formulate his own precepts for a new form of theatre, which he intended would provide the intellectual framework for the eventual production of *Ubu Roi*, by no means certain at the time of writing. This long and detailed piece of dramatic theory was published in the *Mercure de France* as an article entitled 'L'Inutilité du théâtre au théâtre' in September 1896. Here, he advocated that normally fixed pieces of scenery like windows, that had to be opened, or doors that had to be broken down, could be brought in loose, like props. Actors would be masked. Following the precepts of Japanese Noh theatre for a masked actor, Jarry declared that six main positions of the head when facing the audience and six in profile were enough to express every emotion. With the correct lighting, the actor could displace shadows over the whole surface of his mask to achieve changing expressions, he maintained. This is also a principle of the puppet theatre, where the manipulator will use the angle of the lighting to throw the carved planes of the marionette's features into relief. Indeed most of his suggestions follow the rules of puppetry. Jarry contrasted the conventions of the pantomime of the day, what he called 'dreary, incomprehensible gestures' (for instance blowing a kiss to suggest falling in love), with the 'universal' gestures of the puppet theatre. A violent movement backwards causing the marionette to hit its head against the wall is an example of the universal gesture registering surprise or shock, he confides.[14]

Following his own technique for the voice of Ubu, Jarry called not only for a 'special voice' for each role, but that the actor's delivery should be on one note for the whole of the action, in keeping with the rigid lips of his mask. Just as a glove puppeteer will change the position of his hand to indicate an old, hunched person by comparison with a young one with shoulders thrown back, Jarry insisted that actors too should change their entire posture to fit their roles. He spoke vehemently against the convention of letting young women of twenty represent boys of fourteen or so. In this he was at one with Oscar Wilde, who had not wanted the role of the page in his *Salomé* to be played by a woman. Jarry did not think that a woman's figure could ever represent the musculature of a boy and, misogynist as he was, could not repress his disgust at the knowledge that female curves actually produced *milk*. He underlines the word in his article.[15]

A month before the publication of this article Jarry chose his moment to reinforce an audacious suggestion to Lugné-Poe that he had obviously raised before. The director was travelling, and indebted to Jarry not only for forwarding his letters, but for carrying out dozens of small tasks to do with the administration of the theatre. Jarry's suggestion concerns the role of Bougrelas, son of King Wenceslas and Queen Rosamund of Poland, the young warrior hero of *Ubu Roi*, who would finally put Ubu's army to flight:

> Let me tell you why I am convinced about this idea of having a young lad in the role of Bougrelas: I know one in Montmartre who is very good-looking, with amazing eyes and curly locks right down his back. He is thirteen and reasonably intelligent, provided he is given enough attention. It might be a real fillip for *Ubu*, get the old ladies excited and create a bit of a scandal; whatever happens it will make people sit up; it's never been tried before and I do believe that the 'Œuvre' should have the monopoly of all innovations.[16]

This would not be the first time that Jarry would try to use his influence to further someone's career for personal reasons. Years later he would try to get his sister's very mediocre poetry accepted for publication, pretending that she was a talented aristocratic acquaintance rather than a relative. The gorgeous boy in question was apparently a well-known figure in Montmartre and courted by several writers.[17] Lugné-Poe, sensibly, was not swayed by Jarry's argument, but Jarry continued to refer to this boy as Bougrelas.[18] Unlike Wilde, Jarry at least achieved his objective as far as the gender of the eventual actor was concerned.

Monsieur Ubu had made his début in two short pieces, *L'Auto-clète* and *L'Art et la science*, in Jarry's first collection *Les Minutes de*

Sable Mémorial. In the Rennes cycle of playlets Père Hébert's nickname had already suffered a number of distortions. In coining 'Ubu', Jarry changed the characterizing vowel of the name Hébert or Ébé from 'É' to 'U'. This change placed it in a more frightening phonetic family, closer in sound to the ominous hoot of his own beloved owls. In addition to changing the name of his character Jarry made him more powerful, enabling the previously innocuous figure of Père Heb to put himself on the throne of Poland. The Ubu character possesses vices and weaknesses unmitigated by virtues. His immoral behaviour is only kept in check by cowardice. Ubu's Conscience, who appears in *Ubu Cocu* but not *Ubu Roi*, is an entirely separate character kept in a suitcase for occasional consultation, but whose advice is never taken.

The first scene of *Ubu Roi* is devoted to the ambitious Mère Ubu's efforts to persuade her husband, a loyal captain of the Polish Dragoons, to assassinate Wenceslas, King of Poland. Still an innocent with apparently high morals, Ubu protests that he would rather die than commit this treacherous act. Mère Ubu's blandishments prevail, however, and Ubu recruits his officer colleague Captain Bordure to help him carry out his plot. It is interesting that Père and Mère Ubu then switch their moral positions and personalities to some extent. Once King Wenceslas and his sons, Boleslas and Ladislas, have been successfully eliminated, Ubu throws his principles to the wind. It is now Mère Ubu who is the more cautious and sensitive to right and wrong. The youngest prince, Bougrelas, has survived. Mère Ubu realizes that he will seek vengeance. In an interesting (for her) perception that right often triumphs over wrong, she warns her husband that Bougrelas may well win the day as 'he has justice on his side'. She also reminds him of his debt to Bordure. However Ubu has no intention of rewarding Bordure nor, he retorts, does he perceive any difference between justice and injustice. He threatens to chop Mère Ubu up for spoiling his fun.

The scene that follows is one of gruesome slapstick and wonderful theatre. Ubu has assembled specialist accoutrements for dealing with the aristocracy, whose property and wealth he intends to seize. As the aristocrats are brutally pushed forward, it is once more Mère Ubu who tries to stay her husband's hand, but in vain. There is to be no mercy for the aristocrats, whom Ubu will personally seize one by one with his special hook and cast down the hatch into the maw of the debraining machine, a macabre invention that harked back to the Lycée de Rennes.

The Polish judges are next in line. To their credit, they refuse Ubu's offer of living off the fines that they would (unfairly) impose and the property of the people they would condemn to death. For this refusal they are committed to the hatch themselves. Ubu then announces to the treasury officials the various taxes that he intends to impose, of which he will pocket 50 per cent for his own use. The

Alfred Jarry, publicity poster for *Ubu Roi*, 1896.

horrified officials meet the same fate as their predecessors. Ubu is now left alone with Mère Ubu, whom Jarry depicts as appalled by the murderous nature that his new kingly status has brought to the surface. 'Kings aren't supposed to behave like this!' she protests. Misunderstanding why she is upset, he tries to console her by saying he will go from village to village collecting the taxes himself.

The magnificent four-colour publicity poster for *Ubu Roi*, designed and printed by Jarry, encapsulates the scene in which Ubu is engaged in his tax collecting venture, aided by his henchmen, the Palotins. His victims kneel, begging for mercy, their house burns and a winged Palotin, shown here as a bird-balloon with antennae, rises from it with a bag of money in its claws. In one hand, instead of his signature green candle, a towering and barely human Ubu brandishes a torch whose flame curves menacingly over the scene like a macabre reptilian saw. Here it symbolizes Ubu's status as a scourge like Rousseau's figure of *La Guerre*, who also carried a flaming torch. His other hand is a hook on the end of a rolled up arm, clasping a huge money bag, whose corpulence duplicates the curve of his swollen stomach.

This is a different image of Ubu to those so far drawn by Jarry, one that combines greed, avarice and mindless cruelty. Declaring that he is *perhaps* King, in the legend inscribed above his head, Ubu threatens torture, 'decollation' and beheading if his victims do not pay up. No longer ridiculous, Ubu now represents a real, destructive force. It is true that a real tyrant would not go about the country personally collecting taxes;[19] but Jarry's idea was to turn the figure of Ubu into a potent visual symbol of the type of pitiless tyranny that he wanted to satirize. This was very far from the bumbling figure of Père Hébert. The sentiments of Jarry's new monster-tyrant are summed up in the grim motto inscribed between his legs: 'It won't take long to make my fortune, where-upon I shall kill everyone and go away.' This is an expression of greed in its purest form. If Ubu were a lone survivor in a deserted world without people to provide goods and services, money would be useless. Jarry here represents Ubu as a kind of voracious blight, which would indeed vanish having destroyed mankind.

Mère Ubu, for all her aversion to the mass murder that she had witnessed her husband commit, turns out to be cut from the same cloth when it comes to her grasping nature and lust for money. For the early part of the play, Jarry specified that she should wear a pink bonnet or flamboyant hat decorated with both flowers and feathers, such as a shopkeeper-landlady with vulgar taste would wear.[20] As such, she is not so much sinister as comic. She makes her way to Warsaw Cathedral intending to steal the treasure concealed in its crypt before Ubu can get to it. Ubu is fully occupied because Captain Bordure has turned against him and joined forces with the Czar, pledging to restore Bougrelas to the throne. Ubu therefore faces the might of the Russian army.

In an unlikely sequence of events, following the rout of Ubu and the Polish army, the Ubus end up separately taking refuge in a pitch black cave in Lithuania. Jarry uses the darkness to comic effect, but it is a difficult scene to play. To conceal her identity and relying on her husband's stupidity, Mère Ubu pretends to be the voice of the archangel Gabriel. Realizing that she will in the end be found out, she reminds Ubu of his crimes, but tells him that he will be spared if he forgives his wife for 'diverting a small amount of cash'. At first Ubu is duped, but the subterfuge collapses when daylight comes and Mère Ubu is discovered. The furious Ubu threatens her with all the tortures in his repertoire and is actually beginning to tear her to pieces when Bougrelas and his soldiers burst into the cave. There is a spirited hand to hand fight, in which the Palotins join, and which makes for an excellent piece of stage play. Ubu, despite much shouting and bravado, messes his pants but manages to escape. The final scene finds the reconciled Ubus on board a ship bound for France. A storm allows for more slapstick comedy as Ubu attempts to emulate nautical jargon and give orders to steady the ship. Mère Ubu has meanwhile put her political ambitions behind her and declares 'How delightful it will be to see our sweet France once more.' Instead of killing off his tyrant, Jarry decides to defuse him and preserve him for future adventures. Ubu was destined to reappear in *Ubu Enchaîné* and *Ubu Cocu.*

The performance innovations created by Jarry for the play *Ubu Roi* were far more important for theatre history than its plot. In fact, if we are to believe the testimony of Firmin Gémier (likely to be more plausible than Rachilde's 1928 account), it was the performance innovations and the tests to which they subjected the audience's imagination, rather than the vulgarity of the opening word, that caused them to erupt and protest. We know from W. B. Yeats's record of the night that the actors did indeed affect the jerky movements of marionettes: 'The players are supposed to be dolls, toys, marionettes, and now they are all hopping like wooden frogs, and I can see for myself that the chief personage, who is some kind of king, carries for a sceptre a brush of the kind that we use to clean a closet.'

Despite the fact that Yeats joined the claque that was shouting for the play, he went back to his hotel with a feeling of deep sadness, realizing that he had witnessed the end of what he perceived as his own artistic era, one of refined delicacy, and the beginning of a new, more savage one: 'After S. Mallarmé, after Verlaine, after G. Moreau, after Puvis de Chavannes, after our own verse, after the faint mixed tints of Conder, what more is possible? After us the Savage God.'[21] Yeats lamented the growing power of what he called 'comedy and objectivity', but Paris was not yet ready for such a radical perform-ance. Despite Jarry's meticulous preparation, the dress rehearsal and première represented the full extent of *Ubu Roi*'s run. But what an impact it made! As well as Gémier's, Lugné-Poe's and Rachilde's accounts, the critics have left us a fair record on which to draw, although writers differ over which out of the dress rehearsal and the première was the performance at which the uproar took place.

It was apparently unusual for the Œuvre's productions to run beyond the dress rehearsal and the première, so it was not as if *Ubu Roi* was taken off early.[22]

Lugné-Poe's Théâtre de l'Œuvre did not have premises of its own. It was at the Nouveau Théâtre, 15 rue Blanche, that *Ubu Roi* opened at 8.30 pm on 9 December 1896. Pierre Bonnard, Paul Sérusier and Jarry himself spent most of the previous night painting the backdrop. Lugné-Poe recorded that Edouard Vuillard, Paul Ranson, Ker-Xavier Roussel and Toulouse-Lautrec all contributed to it. Jarry had insisted on a static 'eternal' backdrop, representing all climes, times and places to emphasize that the play itself was set in Eternity. Each actor had adopted a 'special voice' according to Jarry's instructions. Louise France played Mère Ubu in *patois*, Bordure had an English accent, the Queen an Auvergnat accent and Gémier imitated Jarry's staccato delivery.

Like Yeats, the writer Arthur Symons was among the foreign tourists in the audience. His account and that of the journalist Robert Vallier more or less agree. On the left stood a four-poster bed with bright yellow curtains and a conspicuous chamber pot, they wrote. Above the bed was a clear blue sky from which snow-flakes were falling. At its foot stood a bare tree festooned with a python. On the right were palm trees and a gallows, complete with dangling skeleton. Through a window painted against the sky could be seen Jarry's hallmark owls and bats flitting above wooded hills. The playwright's speech refers to little elephants grazing on book-shelves. If not these, a single elephant was certainly silhouetted against the red sun that topped the composition. Instead of entering and exiting from the wings, the actors emerged from the fireplace. An elderly actor wearing formal evening dress tiptoed across the stage between every scene and hung up a sign announcing the new location[23] – for example, 'A Cave in Lithuania'. This device avoided having to change the sets, as Jarry had argued in his January letter to Lugné-Poe.

Before the curtain went up a shabby table was carried out, covered with a piece of old sacking. To deliver his introductory speech in front of the footlights, Jarry, pale at the best of times, had put on thick white makeup, but was informally dressed in a sweater and huge bow tie. Even though he took the precaution of reading his speech, the tiny author, used as he was to invisibility and performing behind a screen, was overwhelmed by the occasion and almost lost his voice when it came to addressing the auditorium. We have its text, but his words were inaudible. His discussion of Ubu's provenance, and the esoteric significance of his spherical shape in relation to the arguments of the German philosopher, Dr Misès, were lost on an impatient audience, ready to take part in, or at least witness an outrageous event. Jarry's final sentence, however, did set the tone for what they were expecting: 'The action, which is about to begin, takes place in Poland, that is to say, Nowhere.'[24]

The next word that the audience heard, as Gémier took centre stage was the eagerly awaited '*merdre!*' The various English translations, 'Shittrr!' 'Pschitt!' 'Shite' or 'Crrap' do not have quite the same resonance. None the less, it was a fiction invented by Rachilde that 'the Word' sparked off a riot among the audience. Although Jules Renard's journal recounts a spectator retorting '*mangre*' to Ubu's '*merdre*', none of the contemporary reviews support Rachilde's account. *Ubu Roi* had been in print for six months and the audience knew what to expect. At the dress rehearsal, Gémier recollected, there was laughter for the first two acts, but no disturbance immediately after the opening word. According to him, the problem arose in Act III, scene 5, set at the prison of Thorn, where, instead of rewarding Bordure, Ubu had imprisoned his former loyal captain and arrives to pay him a final, gloating visit.

In the prison scene a single actor was called upon to mime first the prison wall and then the door, the keyhole and the door handle.

Charles-Lucien Léandre, portrait sketch of Jarry reading his preliminary address to *Ubu Roi*, 10 December 1896.

Jarry's radical solution to the many changes of scene against an unchanging backdrop was to have actors standing in for the décor and to create what Romain Coolus called a new theatrical language of signs.[25] This was a bridge too far for an audience unused to such extreme simplification and who felt that their imagination was being unfairly overtaxed. Gémier turned the key in the actor's hand as if it were the lock, imitating the sound of a rusty mechanism, *cric-crac*. He then turned the hand itself to imitate the door handle. It was at this point, Gémier recalled, that pandemonium broke out: 'Cries, insults, gushed out from every corner, with whistles and an accompaniment of other noises – far worse than anything I had ever experienced. I had heard of something similar happening with badly received avant-garde plays, but never had I experienced the sensation that the audience could stop one dead.'[26]

This was also the moment at which André Antoine, director of the 'Naturalist' Théâtre Libre, stood up and shouted: 'This way for the exit!' The playwright, Georges Courteline, also stood up and snapped: 'Don't you see that Jarry is having us on!'[27] To the subsequent dismay of her father, a respected councillor, the wife of the artist Paul Ranson was reported to have been standing on her chair and shouting. Rachilde and Colette's husband, Willy, were meanwhile trying to quieten the uproar, which went on for a full fifteen minutes. To fill the gap Gémier had the inspired idea of dancing a frantic jig, finally collapsing, apparently exhausted, over the prompter's hole. The audience was shocked into silence and then began to applaud him. The actor had won them over and the play was able to continue.[28] The following evening Gémier equipped himself with a megaphone to have a better chance of making himself heard. At the première the play thus came even closer to its puppet origins, the prancing character of Ubu interacting with the vociferous audience in the manner of a Punch and Judy show.

According to the journalist Georges Rémond, Jarry's plan had been to provoke a more dramatic theatrical scandal than those of *Phèdre* and *Hernani*. His personal *claque* were not his literary friends, but drinking companions from his local restaurant, Chez Ernest. They had been briefed to start a disturbance, whatever happened. On the one hand they were to counter any applause with furious shouts, but in the case of boos and whistles, to utter ecstatic cries of delight. They had also been urged to engage in physical fights with their neighbours and to throw whatever missiles they could find into the orchestra pit.[29] According to Rémond, Jarry did not intend the play to reach its conclusion. The audience itself was to provide the theatrical event. This is born out by the fact that he did not preserve any of the favourable reviews of *Ubu Roi*, but carefully compiled a scrap book of adverse criticisms.[30] It is perfectly obvious that the usefulness of the play to Jarry was as a vehicle of provocation and a framework for his theatrical innovations. The text, however much he had revised it and made it his own, was of secondary importance. A critical duel began between Henry Fouquier of *Le Figaro*, who condemned the play as a despicable form of literary anarchism, and Henry Bauer who, putting his reputation on the line, supported it with three long articles in *L'Écho de Paris* of 12 and 19 December. Here is Bauer: 'From this huge, strangely suggestive figure of Ubu, blows the wind of destruction, inspiration of today's youth, which destroys everything that has been traditionally respected and the prejudices of centuries.'

Jarry's disdain for flattery and praise may have been the reason why he had to be prompted to write to thank the eminent journalist, Catulle Mendès, for his wise analysis of Jarry's achievement in creating the Ubu phenomenon:

> A new type has been put before us, created by the extravagant and brutal imagination of a man who is a sort of child.
>
> Père Ubu exists . . .
>
> You will not be able to get rid of him; he will haunt you and perpetually force you to remember not only that he passed this way, but that he has arrived and is here . . . [31]

Jarry had received a similar accolade from Mallarmé, thanking for his presentation copy of *Ubu Roi*, earlier that year:

> With the skill of a sure and sober dramatic sculptor, my dear friend, and with a rare and durable clay upon your fingers, you have set a prodigious figure on his feet, together with his troop.
>
> He enters the repertoire of high taste and haunts me; thank you.[32]

The publication of the book *Ubu Roi*, which might never have reached the consciousness of the wider public, was of course a very different matter to the staging of the play, whose inspiring innovations would be remembered and built upon by avant-garde playwrights and directors during and after the Great War of 1914–18. Apollinaire, Marinetti, Cocteau, Picasso, Ionesco and Beckett each looked to *Ubu Roi* as a model for their experiments. So too did the writers of Zürich's Café Voltaire for the performances of Dada, in particular Jarry's 'sordid' costumes and masks, his use of the raw, brutal dialogue of marital strife and Gémier's recourse to dance and to exchanging insults with the audience.

After such a long passage of preparation for the staging *Ubu Roi*, Jarry was afflicted with the kind of indifference to the fate of their creation that writers often experience in the aftermath of writing a book. With so many free seats given away, Lugné-Poe had been landed with expenses incurred by Jarry without his permission that were no way defrayed by the meagre takings of 1,450 francs. This was his immediate concern. Nor was he sure how the fracas created by *Ubu Roi* reflected on the Œuvre's reputation as a serious theatre. Would it recover? He felt that he had been taken advantage of, if not duped by, Jarry. The relationship between the director and the once so helpful writer would never be quite the same. Jarry too was facing financial ruin. Not only had his months as the Œuvre's administrative secretary been unpaid, but he would not be seeing any benefit from the proceeds of his play. The rents from Laval were not going to support his Paris lifestyle and he would have to seek his income from new writing.

6

'The Rising Light of the Quartier Latin'?

Fame did not mean fortune for Jarry. He did not make any money out of the tumultuous production of *Ubu Roi* and was immediately forced to come to terms with his straitened circumstances. This entailed giving up his spacious flat on the boulevard Saint-Germain and returning to the cramped quarters of the Calvaire du Trucidé at 78 boulevard Port Royal. He did not even have the money to pay the rent, and would face eviction by his previously tolerant landlord in the summer.

In February, on the heels of his move, the Lavallois bicycle merchant Jules Trochon, to whom Jarry owed 525 francs for his up to the minute, deluxe Clément racing bicycle, sent him a final demand through his solicitor. A normal bicycle would have cost about 100 francs at the time, but the astonishing price of the Clément has been confirmed by a longstanding bicycle manufacturer as perfectly reasonable for a custom-made racing bicycle of that date.[1] Did Jarry intend to pay? Never one to economize, he no doubt foresaw a grand future in store for himself, guaranteed by his coming fame. It is true that when he had ordered the bicycle during the preparation of *Ubu Roi* in November 1896, it had a practical purpose. He was making a long uphill journey from his apartment on the boulevard Saint-Germain to the offices of the Œuvre at 22 rue Turgot in Montmartre and his old bicycle would have hardly been up to the task. In frustration Jarry ordered the fastest and most expensive bicycle on the market and then embellished it with wooden wheel rims, also from Trochon. In fact the correspondence with the bicycle merchant, during which Jarry endlessly promised to pay, turned into a saga that would drag on for the rest of his life. The bill for the bicycle, probably his most precious possession and a part of his persona, would never be paid.

A more physical quarrel would shortly be chalked up against Jarry's record. At the end of Rachilde's *mardi* salon, a group had gone to dine at the Taverne du Panthéon on the corner of the rue Soufflot and the boulevard Saint-Michel. Dinner had finished and rather too many liqueurs had been drunk when the sound of a fight suddenly erupted. Christian Beck, the Belgian writer, was allowing himself to be mercilessly pummelled by Jarry, his face contracted with fury.[2] This was the *Mercure* dinner that Gide incorporated into *The Counterfeiters* of 1925. Léon Paschal, who recorded the real event, made no mention of shots. Gide's portrayal of Jarry firing blanks at his victim was probably an amalgamation with the shooting incident with Manolo of 1905. By that time Jarry would be a serious alcoholic, in poor health and considerably more unstable than eight years earlier.

The cause of Jarry's anger towards Beck was never determined. The fact that the writer, six years his junior and once his friend, had succeeded him in the post of secretary-administrator at the Œuvre may not be irrelevant. In August 1896 Beck had written a presumptuous letter to his friend, Paul Gérardy, about the maga-zine that they intended to launch in association with Jarry's *Perhinderion*, publishing coloured engravings on the same lines. He casually assumed that Jarry would bear all the costs and also pass them the list of wealthy subscribers who had previously taken *L'Ymagier*.[3] Beck was certainly not included in the founding of *Perhinderion* and probably underrated Jarry's extreme sensitivity to being exploited. Not satisfied with mere blows, Jarry crystallized his contempt for the unfortunate Belgian into the character Bosse-de-Nage (literally 'bum-face') in his later novel *Faustroll*. Beck's

Arrivée au Phalanstère du jeune Indien (Alfred Jarry dit Ubu.)

Jarry arriving at the Phalanstère on his Clément Luxe bicycle, 1898.

speech impediment and shyness are cruelly characterized by the fact that, throughout the novel, Bosse-de-Nage, a dog-faced baboon, is only able to articulate the two syllables 'Ha ha', whose multiple meanings have been explored by the Collège de 'Pataphysique,[4] but which actually translates as the non-committal 'Uh-huh'.

The Collège de 'Pataphysique (*sic*) was founded in Paris in 1948 by a group of intellectuals as a kind of impudent alternative to the French academic establishment. The Collège was to follow the later definitions of pataphysics formulated by Jarry for his novel *Faustroll*, namely 'the science of imaginary solutions' and 'the science of the particular . . . that will study the laws governing exceptions', . . . 'given', they added, that 'a rule is itself an exception to the exceptional'. In pursuing this science, the College's declared aim was the gathering and furtherance of entirely useless knowledge. Its members also set about collecting and commenting on Jarry's scattered work in publications that continue to appear today.

It was a weakness of Jarry's that he was unable to keep his personal animosities from encroaching on his fiction. This form of revenge was liable to backfire. His colourful and slanderous portraits of Fargue, Courrière and Beck were all now in print. In his private correspondence, he kept his affections in check, but when he felt betrayed or compromised he could not prevent his anger flowing over into his public work.

The most affectionate surviving letter in Jarry's correspondence consists of two sentences and a post scriptum to Claudius-Jacquet, his friend from the Lycée Henri IV, written a month or so before the production of *Ubu Roi*. A unique example of *tutoiement*, it is an anxious reminder. Despite the brevity of the letter, Claudius-Jacquet can have been left in no doubt that Jarry desired his company and that the invitation was not a casual one:

My dear Claudius
Please remember that I'm counting on you for Monday at the 'Œuvre' at three, as you can't make it before Monday. I'll be there tomorrow, Saturday, as well and can't be sure of getting back before 7 o'clock. Couldn't you possibly drop by my flat after 8 o'clock. That way I wouldn't keep you too late.
Your friend
Alfred Jarry
If you can't pass by tomorrow, Saturday, it would be helpful for me to know so that I can assure Fanny and Bougrelas that you are on your way and not be waiting for you on the assumption that you might have been held up. You know that it would give us great pleasure if you can come.[5]

In no other letter does Jarry expose his affections so openly. The variety of alternatives that he offers his friend, in case any one of them should be inconvenient, follows the pattern of the missives written to him by Berthe de Courrière. The polite formula of his final sentence and his mention of the actress Fanny Zaessinger and Bougrelas betray his uncertainty about Claudius-Jacquet's response to an invitation from him alone. No letters from Claudius-Jacquet to Jarry survive, but Jarry's notes and postcards were not thrown away.

At a superficial level, Jarry was held in affection by the Nabi painters who had helped paint the scenery for *Ubu Roi* and by Claude Terrasse, who had composed the music for the play and for the 'Debraining Song', which was enjoying a fame of its own. Having discovered Jarry, Terrasse never let him go. He himself was already in the Nabi 'family' through his marriage to Bonnard's sister, Andrée. The Nabis had taken Ubu to their hearts and now adopted Jarry-as-Ubu into their family. They would make Ubu theirs.

In May 1897 Jarry's novel, *Les Jours et les Nuits, roman d'un déserteur*, was published by the Mercure de France. Apart from the story of Jarry's own army experiences, it is thought to record incidents relating to his friendship with Claudius-Jacquet. It was the last of Jarry's novels that Vallette would publish as a volume. Those who read *Les Jours et les Nuits* searched in vain for the vulgar humour of *Ubu Roi*. In her late review of the book Rachilde attempted to counter the notion of a regressive, nostalgic Jarry and to rescue him from similar accusations. In a metaphorical flourish that alluded to the *Jours* and *Nuits* of the title, but had nothing to do with the escapist theme intended by Jarry, she claimed to perceive 'the huge mask of Monsieur Ubu blocking the light from the narrow window of a better day', hinting at sinister undertones that simply did not exist. Other reviewers confessed to bewilderment. Perceived as a reversion to Symbolist literary practices, the book was not a success. Its literary value would not be appreciated until the 1930s, when André Breton reassessed it in the context of Surrealism's high estimation of dream and the unconscious as vital components of creativity.

Jarry suffered from being a prophet before his time. Hardly prolific, he was excluded from the Mercure de France's *Almanach des poètes pour 1897*. His difficult and dense poetry did not appear in anthologies until after the Second World War, when the Swiss art historian and Dada chronicler, Carola Giedion-Welcker, selected eight of his poems for her collection *Poètes à l'écart*, all but two of which were drawn from *Les Minutes de Sable Mémorial*. She nominated Jarry together with Charles Cros as two of the most important precursors of Dada. Calling her subjects 'poets on the edge', she identified the link between them as 'an extreme need for independence', which led them to overthrow the ethics and aesthetics of their era and their bourgeois background.[6]

Jarry belonged to the small group of poets who were not afraid to experiment with language. His notorious *merdre* and mysterious Pataphysics were only two of his inventions. He also took pleasure in using ambiguous words and constructing similar sounding groups of words, which could be interchanged despite the difference in their conventional meanings. His article 'Ceux pour qui il n'y eut point de Babel' declares his belief in a profound relationship between same-sounding words in different languages.[7] Punning challenges the notion of 'correct' speech and, as a true disciple of Rabelais, it was a practice in which Jarry revelled. His associative technique is a clear precedent for the games played by the Dada group when composing poetry, and the automatic writing practised by the Surrealists. The Surrealists especially admired his chapter, 'Les Propos des Assassins', a real experiment by Jarry and his friends, recounted in *Les Jours et les Nuits*, in which the participants, who have taken hashish, throw similar sounding words and combinations of words backwards and forwards, creating an extraordinary

Jarry photographed by Nadar in 1896.

sequence of images.[8] Jarry disguised the names of his friends through simple oppositional cross-lingual coding. Ernest La Jeunesse became Severus Altmensch and Lord Alfred Douglas became Bondroit.

On 25 April 1897 Rachilde gave a lunch for the artist Aubrey Beardsley at the Lapérouse Restaurant. As her protégé, Jarry's presence at this lunch can almost be guaranteed. Beardsley mentions the occasion in a letter to his sister, Mabel, dated the following day. He complained to her that the 'long-haired monsters of the Quartier' all presented him with 'quite unreadable' books. It is highly probable that Jarry was one of these, although

Beardsley does not single him out by name.[9] Arnaud states that Jarry was introduced to Beardsley by Henry Davray, the Mercure de France's English translator, in April 1897.[10] Davray was also at the lunch, so this is likely to have been the occasion of their meeting.

It would not be surprising if the fastidious Beardsley was put off by the long-haired writer, whose linen was never immaculate and whose trousers may have been mud-spattered from cycling. When Oscar Wilde was introduced to Jarry he wrote an enthusiastic letter to Reginald Turner describing Jarry not only as attractive, but 'the rising light of the Quartier Latin'.[11] No such plaudit has been recorded from Beardsley's side. Nor are Jarry's feelings about the artist clear. It has long been assumed that the chapter that he dedicated to Beardsley in his novel *Faustroll* was a eulogy, following the pattern of most of the other chapters and in tune with contemporary manners.[12] However, the language and tone of the piece throws that interpretation into doubt.

It was also assumed that Jarry's mention of a portrait, *Sieur Faustroll*, by Beardsley, was a real portrait of the author himself, since lost, and not a fictitious one. This would have provided evidence for mutual respect and has been taken as such. A spoof reconstruction of this portrait, published by the Collège de 'Pataphysique, has even been validated in two exhibition catalogues as a genuine Beardsley.[13] If the portrait is to be sought at all, it is important to separate Jarry's fictitious character, Dr Faustroll, from the author himself. Jarry described Dr Faustroll as beardless, but sheathed from groin to toe in black fur like a satyr and 'more of a man than was actually decent'. Was there an existing Beardsley drawing that fitted this description?

One of Jarry's tasks had been to find material for the 'Monsters' section of *L'Ymagier*. He continued the monster theme in *Perhinderion* by reproducing Sebastian Münster's fantastical fifteenth-century woodcuts of aquatic beasts. The illustrations for *Perhinderion* no. 3 were already prepared. If the expense of the first two numbers

de se manifester. Mais le roy voyant que nul ne se monstroit, il enuoya 100. pietons Macedoniens par la riuiere, lesquelz estoyẽt armez à la legiere. Ilz n'eurẽt pas si tost nagé la qua-
triesme partie de ce fleuue, que voicy vne horrible chose & espouantable, qui se presenta de-
uant leurs yeux: a sauoir des cheuaux de riuiere, qu'ilz veirent sortir hors des gouffres pro-

fondz des eaues, & prinrẽt les rustres qui
nageoyent par la teste, & les engloutirẽt
voyãt toute l'armee. Ces bestes se trouuẽt
principalement dedãs le Nil & Ganges:
elles ont les ongles fẽduz cõme en bœuf
le dos, les crainz & le hannillement d'vn
cheual, la queuë torse, & les dentz cro-
chues cõme vn sanglier. Le roy se courrou-
ça lors contre les conducteurs, qui auoiẽt
mené l'armee en telles embusches, & les
feit ietter tous cent cinquante dedãs ceste
riuiere, et ces bestes furieuses les mass acre-
cent, comme ilz auoyent bien merité. Par
cans donc de sa, ilz trouuerẽt sa aupres des
hõmes qui trauersoyent la riuiere sur pe-
tites nasselles faites de ionc. On leur de-
mãda s'il n'y auoit point quelques eaues

douces sa aupres: ilz respondirẽt qu'ilz pourroyẽt trouuer vn grãd estang d'eauë douce, &
leur donneroyẽt des cõducteurs & guides qu'ilz meneroyẽt là sans faillir: toutesfois ilz le
faisoyent à regret. Ilz cheminerent donc toute la nuict, estans accablez & opprimez de soif
& de la pesanteur de leurs armes. Et auec ceste grãde necessité ilz rencontrerẽt d'autres grãs
incõueniens & fascheuses aduentures: ilz eurẽt toute la nuict vne alarme de lyons, ours,
tygres, pardz & lynces, & ainsi leur fallut soustenir vne guerre nouuelle dedans les bois &
forestz. Or cõme la soif les eut amenez à vne grãde necessité, finalemẽt ilz vinrent iusques
à l'estang, enuironné d'vne forest fort espesse, & contenãt mille pas de largeur. Ilz se recrea-
rent là, & y asseirẽt leur campr ilz coupperent le bois, afin que le chemin fust plus facile pour
ceux qui viendroyẽt abreuuer les bestes: & faut biẽ noter qu'il n'y auoit point d'autre estãg
d'eauë douce en toute la regiõ. Ainsi donc entre les pauillons & tentes on dressa des repars
& fortifications, & les elephãs furẽt mis au millieu du cãp: afin qu'ilz se peull entmieux gar-
der de nuict quãd on fust venu pour les surprẽdre, ou s'il fust suruenu quelque bruyt ou crain-
te nouuelle. Il y auoit aussi mille & cinquãte feux allumez par dehors, cõme il auoy't asseez
matiere pour y fournir: afin qu'ilz ne fussẽt soudainemẽt accablez par les habitans du pays.

Sebastian Münster, 'River-horse', a 16th-century woodcut and text from
Cosmographia universalis reproduced in *Perhinderion*, no. 1 (1896).

had not bankrupted him, he had intended to publish three of his own woodcuts, including a new portrait of Monsieur Ubu, an alternative to his earlier 'Véritable Portrait of Monsieur Ubu'.[14] Another modern 'monster' drawn by Beardsley would have been a satisfying complement to this.

In his acceptance of the role of Père Ubu in real life and his impulse to take on the monstrous persona of a caricature, Jarry has been grouped with James Joyce, Georges Rouault and Pablo

Alfred Jarry, variant of the *Véritable Portrait de Monsieur Ubu*, 1896, not published in Jarry's lifetime.

Picasso, who all depicted themselves as clowns in various guises. Rejecting classical notions of beauty, these writers and artists felt impelled to create travesty self-portraits.[15] Did Jarry recognize a similar impulse in Beardsley? The emaciated artist's cover design of a vast-bellied, bejewelled potentate for *Ali Baba and the Forty Thieves* has been identified as a wry, contradictory portrait of himself. In the left hand corner of the drawing his own initials echo the name of the title, *ALI BABA*.[16] This was about to be published when Jarry met him in April 1897. Did Beardsley enjoy drawing subjects with whose names he could identify? If Jarry had been seeking a contemporary drawing of a monster to set beside his

Aubrey Beardsley, 'Alberich' for Wagner's *Das Rheingold*, 1896, ink on paper.

new portrait of Monsieur Ubu, Beardsley's brilliant portrayal of the defiant dwarf Alberich for Wagner's *Das Rheingold*, published in the *Savoy* of December 1896 would have caught his attention. It shows a figure entirely covered in black fur, but for the smooth face and the single upraised fist. It represents a near enough approximation to Jarry's description of Faustroll as 'beardless, but sheathed from groin to toe in black fur'.

None the less, Jarry's inclusion of 'a portrait of Sire Faustroll by Aubrey Beardsley' among the pictures and books confiscated from Faustroll by the bailiff was probably intended to mislead.[17] He gives it credibility by placing it in company with Toulouse-Lautrec's *Jane Avril* and Bonnard's *Revue blanche* posters, both well known. Although it is dangerous to conflate Faustroll with Jarry himself here, it would be reasonable to assume that he might have pinned a Beardsley print from the *Savoy* on his wall. The troll-like features, with which Beardsley endowed his stunningly ugly Alberich, make a strong case for this drawing's candidacy as the missing 'portrait of Sire Faustroll'.[18] Having donned the mask of Ubu himself, Jarry may have felt some fellowship with Aubrey/Alberich, depicting himself as repulsive beast and society outcast, breaking free of his bonds in this illustration.

Each dedicatee of Jarry's novel, *Gestes et opinions du docteur Faustroll, pataphysicien* is allocated an 'island' or 'territory' moulded into an imaginary landscape, with features that the author perceived to be most characteristic of their literature or art. Thus Mallarmé is Master of the Island of Ptyx, after his famous poem with rhymes in *-yx*, while Gauguin is King of the Fragrant Isle, after his Tahitian narrative, *Noa Noa*, meaning 'fragrant'. The chapter that Jarry dedicated to Beardsley is titled 'The Country of Lace' after the extreme delicacy of his dotted line drawings, so suited to depicting the lacy fabrics which swathed many of his subjects.

The cryptic language of 'The Country of Lace' is meticulously constructed to form one of Jarry's most ambiguous texts. If Beardsley was a master of concealment in his drawings, Jarry here demonstrates that he can match his sly visual signals with verbal ones. The homage to Beardsley's graphic technique is real, but the end of the chapter suggests that the artist is in the toils of deep distress. As the illustrator of Wilde's *Salome*, Beardsley had been closely associated with him, but then sought to distance himself from the writer. Charged with multiple acts of gross indecency, Wilde had publicly spoken out in defence of the love between men 'that dare not speak its name'. Jarry's peculiar description of 'the *patient* host' of Beaux and Belles in 'The Country of Lace', and to the 'cry' which scattered them, may well refer to Wilde's eloquent words at his trial on this forbidden subject.[19] Although he was given bail after the hung jury of this first trial, he was subsequently convicted and jailed amid enormous publicity. His friends fled to France. Beardsley's fearful attempts to avoid contact with the tainted writer after his release had hurt Wilde. He is reported to have thought that Beardsley snubbed him in Dieppe by not turning up to a dinner and described his behaviour as *lâche* (cowardly).[20] He may have said as much to his Mercure de France friends. The text of 'The Country of Lace', published in the *Mercure de France* journal in May 1898, should be considered in the context of Jarry's own warm meeting with Wilde a mere month earlier.

When he dedicated two chapters to the warring Gauguin and Bernard in *Faustroll*, Jarry had been evenhanded in his homage. Separating the two artists, by place rather than primacy, he allocated Bernard dominion over Pont-Aven's *Bois d'Amour* for his *Bretonneries* series and religious paintings, and made Gauguin King of the *Fragrant Isle*, for his Tahitian paintings and carvings. In dedicating a chapter to Beardsley he could have balanced it with one to Wilde. He did not do so. It seems that he did not dare publish an outright tribute to him. His solution was to conceal allusions to Wilde's *Salome* within the ambiguous chapter dedicated to Beardsley, creating a far from unmitigated tribute to the artist.

It is the textual oddities of 'The Country of Lace' that cast its superficial character as a tribute into doubt. Any notion as to fixity of meaning must be abandoned. Each word or word part must be regarded as an independent entity, and subjected to Jarry's personal rule, that words from different languages that sound the same share a similar meaning.[21] The words in this chapter should be analysed not only in the context of the French language, but in the context of Beardsley's native English. Even as we step into the so-called 'pure' light of 'The Country of Lace' we should do so with care. In his novel *L'amour absolu*, written at the same date, Jarry uses the word 'pureté' (purity) as if it were in the same linguistic family as the word 'puant' (stinking).[22] So the reader should be warned that, coming from his pen, the word 'pure' contains an element of stinking rottenness.

In describing 'The Country of Lace', Jarry's style is at first chatty and colloquial as he describes known and innocuous Beardsley drawings, such as his *Madonna and Child* Christmas card and the Rhine Maidens of *Das Rheingold*. The reader can perceive a recognizable Beardsley landscape. But suddenly the syntax and the language change to an antiquated style, laden with complex comparative clauses. This change signals the writer's withdrawal into a private world of reference. The emphasis also switches from the visual to the aural. As instructed in Jarry's preface to *Les Minutes de Sable Mémorial*, the reader must weigh this piece 'in the scales of his ears'. Jarry evokes protesting cries and screams, a Pierrot singing to the moon and a howling Ali Baba. Both are Beardsleyan subjects, but neither matches any of the artist's known pictures. The passage is so full of words signifying deceit and discordance (my italics) that the reader should beware of taking it at face value:

The Beaux and the Belles strutted about and swept backwards and forwards in *imitation* of fans, until their patient throng scattered with a cry of alarm. Just as white peacocks, roosting in a park, clamour *discordantly* when the *lying intrusion* of a torch flame prematurely *apes* the dawn, their mirror, a white shape bulged in the scratched pitchy black of the thicket; and as Pierrot sings to the *confused tangle* of the balled up moon, the *paradox* of a minor day dawning rose from Ali-Baba howling in the pitiless oil and the opacity of the jar.[23]

Here the clause about the white peacocks and their cries seems mysteriously inappropriate to the development of the main sentence. Where do they fit in? The baffled reader may well rack his brains in the hope that a recognizable Beardsley drawing might emerge from the confusion. He is bracketed with the ape, Bosse-de-Nage, who can only utter 'Ha ha!' We are told that Bosse-de-Nage understood little of these prodigies and did not dwell on them any further. By implication, the reader is urged to move on.

The literary origin of Jarry's allusion to white peacocks in a park is surely Wilde's *Salome*, illustrated by Beardsley. His tortuous comparative clause would then refer to the most lyrical and dramatic passage in the play, where Herod, desperately attempting to divert Salome from her request for John the Baptist's head, offers her his prized flock of white peacocks:

Salome, thou knowest my white peacocks, my beautiful white peacocks, that walk in the garden between the myrtles and the tall cypress-trees. Their beaks are gilded with gold and the grains that they eat are smeared with gold, and their feet are stained with purple. When they cry out the rain comes, and the moon shows herself in the heavens when they spread their tails . . . I will give thee fifty of my peacocks. They will follow thee whithersoever thou goest, and in the midst of them thou wilt be like unto the moon in the midst of a great white cloud . . . I will give them to thee, all.[24]

At the beginning of the novel *Faustroll*, Dr Faustroll had warned the bailiff, Panmuphle, that between the lines of his seized books there were some people who had escaped his so-called 'law' and 'justice', whom he would be taking on board his skiff.[25] Wilde is a candidate for those between-the-lines people whom he smuggles on board and Herod's white peacocks from *Salome* are the fauna that Jarry places in Beardsley's *Country of Lace*.

Our final glimpse of 'The Country of Lace' is of Ali Baba howling as he drowns in the 'pitiless oil'. By placing Beardsley/Ali Baba in the jar, Jarry reverses the real ending of the Ali Baba story, in which Ali Baba's servant performs the lethal pouring of the oil over the robbers hiding in the jars: 'Relentlessly she poured the boiling oil through the mouth (of the jar) on the thief's head, so that he swallowed death with the cry which rose to his lips.'[26] Jarry was the reviewer for *La Revue blanche* of seven of the volumes of Mardrus' translation of *Mille nuits et une nuit* and refers to both Galland's and Richard Burton's previous translations. His reversal of the ending of one of the best known tales must be deliberate. Was he reproaching Beardsley for the cowardly way that he had disassociated himself from Wilde in the wake of the scandal?

It is possible that Jarry's critique reaches even deeper than a reproach for disloyalty to a friend. Beardsley had allowed shallow bourgeois standards and commercial arguments to direct which of his drawings should be published, repeatedly agreeing to more anodyne alternatives. Jarry compares Beardsley to a rope maker teasing out his *ligne rétrograde* (retrograde line).[27] This is surely not a casual choice of words, but an accusation of retrogressiveness. Unlike Wilde, Beardsley had betrayed his artistic integrity and succumbed to the very hypocrisy he had attacked.

If it is indeed Aubrey Beardsley, alias Ali Baba, whom Jarry portrays as immersed in the 'pitiless' boiling oil, like the corrupt clergy of Dante's *Inferno*, it would be on the repression of his artistic integrity and the denial of his genius that Jarry judged him. It would be the suppressed artistic spirit of Beardsley that was howling, not in the Catholic Hell, which Beardsley feared, but a special Hell for artists who had betrayed their calling. In Pont-Aven, Gauguin had propagated Wagner's message calling for a new brotherhood of artists: 'He who submits to an external necessity instead of an internal necessity subjects himself to a constraint . . . he is not free, he is a slave, he is unfortunate.'[28] Beardsley's cowardice would have condemned him to the opposite of Wagner's vision of a special Heaven for artists. It was as near as Jarry would get to a condemnation of an artist whose early subversive work he had admired for its courageous disregard of bourgeois prudishness. Beardsley had died on 16 March 1898. Anything other than a tribute would have been inappropriate, but it is noteworthy that he did not offer this piece as an obituary for Beardsley as he did his homage 'The Island of Ptyx' for Mallarmé.[29]

Jarry predicted that his novel, *Gestes et opinions du docteur Faustroll, pataphysicien*, would not be published in full 'until the author had acquired enough experience to savour all its beauties', that is, until after his death. His prediction was correct. Chapters VI and X to XXV appeared in the May 1898 issue of the *Mercure de France*. The full manuscript was eventually published by Eugène Fasquelle, but not until 1911, four years after Jarry's death.

In August 1897 Jarry had been evicted from the Calvaire du Trucidé. He transformed this grim experience into fiction, inventing the character of Faust-troll, his fictitious counterpart and a gnome in both senses of the word, who suffers the same fate, but who sets off in a boat, in fact a Jumblies-style sieve, 'from Paris to Paris by sea'. In 1894 Henri Rousseau had helped Jarry move from 78 boulevard Port Royal to the boulevard Saint-Germain. Now that Jarry was being evicted from his old lodgings, he offered the near destitute writer a place in his own bed. His last surviving child, Henri-Anatole, had died at the age of eighteen only six months before. Jarry took

Henri Rousseau in 1895.

his place and gave the artist's address at 14 avenue du Maine as his
own until the end of the year.[30] Rousseau's circumstances were
hardly better than Jarry's, but his domestic skills were more
developed. It was known that he cooked on a Tuesday. Jarry,
together with the other down-and-outs of the district benefited
from his Tuesday stews.

Although chapter 32 of *Faustroll*, 'How to get hold of canvas', is
dedicated to Bonnard, it is Rousseau who is here incorporated into
the Faustrollian world. Jarry perceived his middle-aged friend as a
great innovator, whose apparently simple, childlike paintings relied
on an unsophisticated vein of inspiration. Faustroll sends Bosse-de-
Nage to the Musée du Luxembourg (here called 'Le Luxe bourgeois'),
with enough gold to buy up all the academic paintings. In the course
of his mission he is instructed to perform all kinds of bows and
genuflections in the small room devoted to Monet, Degas, Whistler,
Cézanne, Renoir and Puvis de Chavannes' *Poor Fisherman*. He finally
returns with eleven scenery vans full of canvases. Faustroll reveals
that he has turned the gold, now in the pockets of the museum

officials, into the yellow liquid excreted by babies. Faustroll fills
the Painting Machine with this unusual form of *merde* and gives
Rousseau the task of overpainting the canvases with it. The artist
duly points the nozzle of the machine at the academic paintings
and, in Jarry's words, carefully covers them 'with the calm uniform
of chaos'. Why Jarry mentions that he spent 63 days on this task
is not clear. Arnaud speculated that it was the length of time that
Rousseau spent on a particular painting, while he was staying
with him.[31]

During his penurious year of 1897 Rachilde once more tried to
come to Jarry's rescue. Whether or not Gourmont was to blame,
Vallette had closed the doors of the Mercure de France to any new
work of Jarry's. Rachilde herself was a prolific, not to say popular
writer. The dense, convoluted prose of *César-Antechrist* had exasperated her. 'Why can't you write like everyone else?' she asked
him. According to her, Jarry said 'Show me how'. Jarry's next novel,
L'Amour en Visites, was the result of this supposed collaboration.
Rachilde claimed to have written one of the chapters, titled 'Fear
pays a call on Love', gently making fun of Jarry's extreme reticence
in matters of the heart. As if the rift with Gourmont were not serious
enough, another of the chapters, 'At home with the *Vieille Dame*',
targeted Berthe de Courrière, publishing her agonizingly embarrassing letters to Jarry word for word. Arnaud speculates that the
pornography publisher Pierre Fort (no relation of Paul) had pressed
Rachilde to publish one of her novels with him and that Rachilde
had thought to do both men a favour by offering him Jarry's *L'Amour
en Visites* instead.[32] Fort did publish the book, but it was hardly in
the interests of Jarry's reputation and nearly landed him in court.
Rachilde's judgement in this matter is questionable.

Meanwhile, the Nabis and other friends had not forgotten
Jarry and were about to come to his rescue. Writing was not the
only talent that he possessed; his skill as a puppeteer was of great
importance to the Nabis. At the very end of the year, on 8 December,

Jarry received a letter from Terrasse: 'Alphonse Hérold is coming to lunch. We need to talk marionettes urgently – all of us together – the theatre is ready.'[33] The prospective theatre was a small pentagonal atelier no more than 40 to 45 square metres large, which stood in the garden behind Terrasse's house at 6 rue Ballu.[34] The Nabis' earlier marionette theatre, the Théâtre des Nabis, was about to be succeeded by the Théâtre des Pantins, with Jarry taking charge of the manipulation and the performance mechanics.

7

From Puppets to Pataphysics

The Théâtre des Pantins was an extraordinary venture, uniting some of the most talented writers, actors and artists of the avant-garde. Opening on 28 December 1897 and closed by the censor at the end of March 1898, well before it had completed its intended programme, it had a short, effervescent life span. Mostly young, those involved were bound by friendship to each other and by affection for Jarry. Brothers and sisters, husbands and wives, they threw themselves into the enterprise with passion. The language of their productions cheerfully broke the bounds of conventional decency, and the performances drew an enthusiastic intellectual audience of their young peers.

Terrasse does not make it clear in his note to Jarry what role Alphonse Hérold, an illustrator of fine books, was to play in the construction of the new puppet theatre, but Jarry would later dub him *celui qui meublait* ('he who provides the furniture').[1] The performances of the Théâtre des Nabis, predecessor to the Théâtre des Pantins, had often taken place in Madame Hérold's attic. Her two sons, Alphonse and André-Ferdinand, were therefore no newcomers to the practicalities of puppetry. Both the Hérold brothers would be closely involved in the Pantins. André-Ferdinand, the orientalist, who was one of Jarry's more frequent companions, had stepped in to take charge of the lighting for the *Ubu Roi* production.

It was Franc-Nohain, however, who was the true instigator of the Pantins project, as his letters to Terrasse reveal.[2] He, Ranson and Jarry were among the very few 'literary' or writer-puppeteers of their age, as opposed to the pavement puppeteers who tended to inherit their repertoire and trade secrets from older family members. Jarry was the main manipulator of the Pantins puppets, but Franc-Nohain and Ranson assisted him. The Bonnard brothers, Pierre and Charles, took on the manufacture of the puppets – apparently a staggering 300 in all[3] – whose heads were moulded from a kind of mastic. Their sister Andrée provided the piano accompaniment, together with her husband, Terrasse, who also composed the music. It had to be a profit-making venture this time, for it was partly conceived as a benefit for Jarry himself. Georges Roussel, brother of the Nabi painter, Ker-Xavier, took on the job of accountant and theatre manager, earning Jarry's title of *celui qui pantinait*. A substantial subscription of 50 francs was proposed as the price of the combined ticket which would admit the holder to all ten productions envisaged for the first season.[4]

Pierre Bonnard, 'Le Théâtre des Pantins', 1898, pencil and wash drawing in *La Vie du Peintre*.

On 21 December, just in time for Christmas, Jarry acknowledged receipt of 75 francs from the theatre administration, of which 50 francs constituted an advance.[5]

All the painters involved in the Pantins project had previously supported both Paul Fort's Théâtre d'Art and its successor the Théâtre de l'Œuvre. They had given their talent and their time to painting the scenery for one production after another. Now that relationship had been broken. In the summer of 1897 Lugné-Poe, disappointed with what he took to be the fracas of *Ubu Roi* and the lukewarm reception of his other French productions, had turned his back on French dramatists and the French Symbolist movement. He published a manifesto declaring that the Œuvre would, from then on, restrict itself to producing plays written by foreign dramatists, as French writers were incapable of producing a masterpiece. This prompted an indignant reply, drawn up by Pierre Quillard and signed by twelve writers, including Jarry. They refused to accept the Symbolist label for three of the French productions he had put on and accused Lugné-Poe of such great condescension towards French writers that the 'relations' he sought to break off with them were 'purely fictitious'. They further declared that Symbolism – if Symbolism existed – had nothing to do with the director, who was simply 'an organizer of theatre performances', in their words.[6] The angry exchanges continued through the press for over a month.

The 'literary' puppet theatres of the 1890s were born of the Symbolist movement. The puppet, almost a symbol in itself, was considered a truer vehicle for the writer's words than the human actor. Jarry was one of the main opponents of the cult of star actors. He expressed his views when he was invited to the Libre Esthétique in Brussels in 1902 to lecture on the Pantins:

> We don't know why we are always irritated by what is generally known as the Theatre. Is it because we know that the actor, however brilliant, betrays the intentions of the poet – and the

more brilliant and individual he is, the worse he does so? Only marionettes, of whom one is sovereign master and Creator, for it seems indispensable to us to have manufactured them oneself, will passively translate the rudimentary framework of one's thoughts, in their bare exactitude.[7]

Lugné-Poe's anti-Symbolist manifesto was a rebuff to Paul Fort, whose Théâtre d'Art he had taken over, also to his French authors and the painters who had helped him, particularly Bonnard and Vuillard, whose atelier he had once shared. The Théâtre des Pantins provided a new focus for their energies. The enterprise was clearly enjoyed by all the participants. A.-F. Hérold catches the atmosphere:

We didn't put on very many plays, but we had a good time. At the Pantins, the modelling of the puppets and the painting of the scenery was carried out by Bonnard, by Vuillard, Ranson and Roussel, who were only appreciated by a very few amateurs at the time. Jarry was holding the strings; Terrasse was at the piano; good-hearted friends read the parts and sang the songs. We played *Ubu Roi*, unabridged; Burgundy nativity plays and a piece by Monsieur Franc-Nohain, *Vive la France*, for which Terrasse had written songs, choruses and even ballet music.[8]

Whereas pavement puppeteers, apprenticed from childhood, relied on a combination of skills handed down from father to son and put on their shows with the help of family members alone, the 'literary' puppet theatres, such as Henri Signoret's Petit Théâtre des Marionnettes and the Pantins, needed to draw on a huge pool of separate actors and artists. It was unusual for a writer from the intellectual elite to become a proficient puppet manipulator and sculptor. A letter from Franc-Nohain to Terrasse proves that Jarry had reached a high level of skill in manipulating stringed mario-nettes. In his letter Franc-Nohain pressed Terrasse to compose

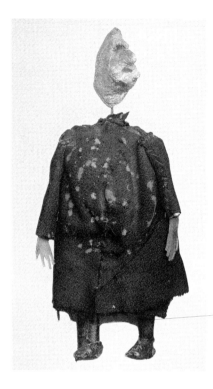

Alfred Jarry, original Père Ubu stringed marionette, 1897, plaster and cloth.

some music for a grand ballet scene to close the second act of his play, *Vive la France!* He was confident that Jarry's 'agile fingers' could manipulate six ballet dancers in tutus, executing five whole minutes of pirouettes in what must have been an extraordinarily difficult manoeuvre.[9]

The Pantins only managed to put on three productions before the censor closed down the theatre. The first was on 28 December 1897, *Paphnutius,* a tenth-century mystery play by the German poetess-nun Hroswitha, translated and adapted by A.-F. Hérold. Next came the reprise of *Ubu Roi* on 20 January 1898. Jarry had sculpted the head of Père Ubu himself. He provided the voice of Ubu, as usual, and Louise France that of Mère Ubu. Fanny Zaessinger, a faithful

Edmond Couturier, 'Alfred Jarry conduisant *Ubu Roi*', in *La Critique*, 5 April 1903.

friend to Jarry, provided the voices of both Queen Rosamund and Captain Bordure. Alas, whereas the Œuvre had been exempt from censorship in its capacity of a 'private' subscription theatre, the Pantins was not. Jarry had to submit his text to the censor, who demanded the deletion of every single *merdre*.[10] Jarry's suggested substitutes *Sangsurdre* or *Mais* were also rejected. The meaningless half word *–Dre* was accepted as the third alternative and, although Jarry preferred to opt for silences at the censored points, the play then enjoyed a run of at least seven performances between 25 and 31 January.[11] It is thought that the suppression of 'the Word' may have given Jarry the idea for the opening of *Ubu Enchaîné* when Ubu refuses to pronounce it.[12]

The Pantins repertoire was ribald by comparison with that of Signoret's and Bouchor's Petit Théâtre. Signoret's repertoire included Aristophanes, Cervantes and Shakespeare, and his delicate rod puppets were based on Javanese precepts. The purpose of the Pantins marionettes was satirical and their crude features were exaggeratedly grotesque. Franc-Nohain composed bawdy songs that made the dialogue of *Ubu Roi* appear almost prim. In true puppet show tradition the audience would join in the refrains with gusto and much laughter. With the death in 1897 of Rodolphe Salis and the closure of his nearby Chat Noir, the Pantins provided a welcome, but all too rare alternative for the intellectual elite to let off steam.

Censorship was to prove the doom of the enthusiastic venture. *Paphnutius* and *Ubu Roi* needed little adaptation, but the new pieces on the programme needed much more preparation. First in line was Franc-Nohain's *Vive la France!*, in which God and the Avenging Angel travel to France in the guise of tourists. More complex was *Les Silènes*, Jarry's adaptation of the comedy *Scherz, Satire, Ironie und tiefere Bedeutung* by Christian-Dietrich Grabbe, a short-lived German writer with whom he felt a strong affinity. At the end of March, banned by the censor and open only to subscribers and friends by private invitation, *Vive la France!* was performed as the

Pantins' closing performance. Jarry had to wait three years for an invitation to Brussels before he had the opportunity to perform excerpts from *Les Silènes* to a paying audience. (The full text of his translation was not performed until 2000, and then not with stringed marionettes, but with table puppets and amateur actors from the Collège de 'Pataphysique.) Bonnard's puppets would have one more outing at 6 rue Ballu for a Pantins retrospective on 10 March 1900. This occasion seems to have been more in the nature of a party for friends than a formal performance. Terrasse recorded that the post-performance dinner went on until 5.30 a.m.[13]

Away from the intense activity of the Pantins, what was happening in Jarry's private life? He was now twenty-four. Most of his friends were already married. The Nabis had adopted him into their 'family' group but, with the closure of the Pantins, that was now dissolving. Happily for him, a project was forming that would give him a healthier bolthole than the narrow confines of the Calvaire du Trucidé, bind him into a different group and allow him to indulge his extraordinary talent as an angler.

Vallette and Jarry had already started canoeing together the previous summer, when Jarry had acquired a mahogany canoe or *as*. Enthused by this new hobby, Vallette and Rachilde conceived a plan to rent a riverside property, which they could share with several like-minded writer friends and where they could take their daughter, Gabrielle. Apart from the Vallettes and Jarry the group would consist of the Greek scholar and anarchist Pierre Quillard, A.-F. Hérold and Marcel Collière, all contributors to the *Mercure de France* journal, but whose friendship went back to the Lycée Fontanes. Characterizing themselves as wild and wicked river beings, they referred to themselves as 'trolls'. Although Faustroll's *as* was actually a sieve, Jarry's riparian existence with his friends must have given him some of the inspiration for his novel.

The Vallettes finally rented a villa near Corbeil on the Seine south of Paris. It was immediately named the Phalanstère. This was a

Utopian concept invented by the philosopher Charles Fourier to designate a place where a community lived and worked together for mutual benefit. Jarry's contribution was to provide fish. He had a knack for catching pike and gudgeon in spots where others failed. One of his few surviving paintings is a tiny landscape on wood commemorating 'The Little Tree', in whose shade he used to fish. In a letter to Vallette he reports catching 39 gudgeon between midday and two o'clock. Henry Davray addresses him in a letter as 'cher Ubu Nautile' and his friends begin to think of him in terms of his riverside existence.

The Vallettes needed to be in Paris during the week so Jarry acted as caretaker for most of the period from spring to December, a period that probably represents the happiest and calmest in his adult life. He took advantage of the peace of the villa to complete his first draft of *Faustroll* early in the year. He writes to Rachilde asking when she is thinking of coming and, knowing her love of animals, teases her, pretending that, as the nightingales had been disturbing

Vallette and Jarry carrying their skiff along the riverbank in 1898.

him, he had shot them – a most unlikely feat.[14] The *Mercure de France* journal published Jarry's initial version of *Faustroll* in their May number. Later he would add more chapters. At the same time, Pierre Fort brought out the very different *L'Amour en Visites* with its slanderous chapter on Berthe de Courrière.

The letter from Davray, dated 18 May 1898, invited Jarry to a meeting with Oscar Wilde, newly in Paris after his release from Reading Gaol the previous year:

> My dear Ubu Nautile,
> O. Wilde has promised to be at the Café Rohan, Place du théâtre français tomorrow, in the hope that you'll be there – I will be – just for the sake of the formal introductions.
> Devotedly yours
> Henry D. Davray[15]

It was short notice, but this was not a meeting that Jarry would have dreamed of missing. What Davray's letter does not tell us is that this momentous meeting was arranged for the first anniversary of Wilde's release, which had taken place on 19 May 1897. Davray's intention was to withdraw so that Wilde could enjoy Jarry's company alone, but it seems from a letter Wilde wrote the following day that Alfred Douglas may have spoiled the occasion by turning up uninvited with an unwelcome companion. Wilde wrote that Davray had invited him to a café to meet a poet who desired to meet him, but that Douglas, 'without the smallest iota of social tact', had thrust an offensive young boyfriend into what was supposed to be a literary reunion.[16] The events of the rest of the evening are unrecorded. However, in a letter to Reginald Turner postmarked 25 May, Wilde wrote that Jarry had sent him 'a complete collection of his works'. If true, this would have amounted to four volumes, apart from *Faustroll*. Wilde's pseudonym, Melmoth, appears on Jarry's lists for complimentary copies of both *L'Amour en Visites* and *L'amour absolu*.[17]

Wilde was charmed by Jarry, whom he called 'a most extraordinary young man' – a rare compliment from his lips. 'In person he is very attractive', he wrote, 'he looks like a very nice renter'.[18] 'Renter' was the word that Wilde used to refer to a male prostitute, but his description of Jarry is one of the most flattering on record. Their encounter was obviously a success. According to Arnaud, they were later seen together at the Bar Calisaya on the boulevard des Italiens, but he does not specify if it was this same evening or another one.[19] Jarry's only direct mention of Wilde is a passing reference to the 'Wilde–Douglas affair' in an article of 1903 for the *Canard sauvage* titled 'An open mind to ancient art'.[20] In that article he examined a parallel to the Wilde case, that of a young poet, Jacques d'Adelsward-Fersen, and was not shy about revealing that his sympathies were with the accused. In an earlier article, 'On various kinds of legal rape', he had already criticized the legal practice of examining children for signs of sexual interference, placing it on a par with criminal rape.[21] 'The magistrates and official doctors', wrote Jarry, 'certainly examined Mr Jacques d'Adelsward much more closely than he explored any of his "victims"'. Familiar as he was with the Montmartre scene, where more than one Bougrelas plied his trade, Jarry objected to the term 'victim', asserting that there was no young 'professional' who, in order to put his client at ease, would not pretend to be eighteen or more. Jarry's two articles, written in the wake of a rape and a sodomy case respectively, focused on what he perceived to be the hypocrisy of legal practice. In his article on what he calls 'legal rapes', Jarry argued that the Law favours anything that is a majority movement, but detests an isolated human being acting on his own. Wilde's solitary stand in favour of 'the Love that dares not speak its name' was of course in the latter category.

In 1897 Jarry had not yet embarked on researching his novel, *Messaline, roman de l'ancienne Rome*, for which he immersed himself in *moeurs antiques*, both heterosexual and homosexual. If his 1903 article is his only direct reference to Wilde, there is nevertheless reason to suspect that he included a disguised homage to Wilde as a Roman emperor in *Messaline*, published shortly before Wilde's death in November 1900. The intention of the poem in question is not accessible to the general reader but would have been apparent to Wilde himself, just as Fargue had been able to recognize himself in *Haldernablou.*

The trip to see Wilde was one of several that Jarry made between Paris and Corbeil during April, May and June, often with A.-F. Hérold. It was only in the latter half of 1898 that he took up residence at the Phalanstère for a continuous period. Many writers and artists spent their weekends in the area. The Belgian writer, Eugène Demolder, staying at the Demi-Lune, the magnificent villa of his father-in-law, Félicien Rops, would often come upstream to fish with Jarry and go drinking in the local bars.

Jarry was one of the local visitors who gravitated to Mallarmé's house at Valvins, as Misia Sert, then wife of Thadée Natanson, editor of *La Revue blanche*, recalled. At this time Jarry was not yet a contributor to the magazine but was often invited to the Natansons in the company of his painter friends, for whom the beautiful Polish pianist was both hostess and muse. Misia later married the millionaire Alfred Edwards – an extraordinary deal, whereby Edwards offered to buy Natanson's bankrupt magazine if he would give up his wife. Misia's fondness for Jarry was no doubt the reason that Edwards tied up his luxury steamer near Jarry's later shack and invited him on board. The story goes that Jarry raised his glass and toasted his host, whereupon Edwards reproached him that toasting was only done in vulgar company. 'That's why I'm doing it', retorted Jarry. In an affectionate, if patronizing reminiscence, Misia remembered him in the context of his riverside existence and his shoes. 'I was fond of that charming little clown who lived by his fishing rod and used to wear Madame Vallette's laced boots.'[22] Misia also recorded that Jarry had ruined some velvet slippers of

Rachilde's while cycling to dinner at Octave Mirbeau's villa.[23] In fact he is only known to have borrowed her yellow laced boots for the occasion of Mallarmé's funeral.

At only 56, the great poet's premature death after sudden attacks of breathlessness on 8 and 9 September 1898 was a terrible shock to the writers who had, for so long, looked to him for a lead. It marked the end of the Symbolist era. Jarry had developed his own poetic method according to the Mallarméan model of maximum suggestiveness, and was similarly interested in typographical experiments. He had looked for Mallarmé's approval, sending him each of his books as it came out. The letters of thanks that he received were, without fail, sensitive and appreciative, praising him for breaking new ground. Mallarmé's *mardis* clashed with Rachilde's and Jarry's attendance at the rue de Rome was rare, but Jarry's friend Dr Albert Haas recalled that on one occasion they both stayed at Mallarmé's house until two o'clock in the morning, listening to him discoursing on the structure of the sonnet.[24] Mallarmé gave nothing but encouragement to his young admirer and the impact of his death on Jarry should not be underestimated.

Mallarmé's funeral took place on 11 September 1898 at the Church of Samureau on the other side of the Seine from Valvins. The critic Édouard Dujardin wrote that he was proud to walk at Jarry's side in the funeral procession.[25] Jarry now extended 'The Isle of Ptyx', his tribute to Mallarmé in *Faustroll*, into an obituary piece which appeared in the *Almanach du Père Ubu, illustré* the following year.[26] In this he does assume Faustroll's identity. He wrote that Mallarmé had read and appreciated the story of Faustroll's voyage. He also wrote that Mallarmé rose from his rocking chair one final time, his hand stretched out towards the doctor. This may or may not mean that Jarry himself had had the chance to see the poet and hear his appreciation of *Faustroll* at first-hand. It may be an entirely imaginary farewell scene in the same vein as his evocation of Beardsley's portrait. When we enter the realm of Dr Faustroll, yellow-skinned and hairy, with sea green moustachios and whose eyes are two ink capsules flecked with golden spermatazoa, we leave the realm of reality. In Jarry's fictionalized account of Mallarmé's funeral, Faustroll walked to Valvins barefoot. Jarry himself had arrived by bicycle,[27] and was seen removing a pair of filthy, worn out shoes, before extracting Rachilde's shining yellow ankle boots from his pocket to take part in the funeral procession.

Jarry had originally hoped that *Gestes et opinions du docteur Faustroll, pataphysicien* would be published by the Mercure de France. It is a fascinating and dense work in which he takes the reader to the worlds of other writers and artists that shaped his own literature. Here too he develops his conception of pataphysics. He gives two parallel lists: the 27 books most important to him, to be taken on board the skiff; and the *élus* or *chosen ones*, 27 poetic items invented by their writers, for which he had a special affection or even borrowed. Jarry's system of preferences is not always straightforward. Sometimes the chosen item is from a different book to the one Faustroll takes on board his skiff.[28] For example Jarry chooses to save Maurice Maeterlinck's play *Aglavaine et Selysette*, yet Faustroll's *élu* from this author is the delightfully contradictory item of 'heard light'. It is taken from Mélisande's song in *Pelléas et Mélisande*, where three blind sisters are climbing a tower, each carrying a lamp, when the first one suddenly cries 'I can hear our lights'. The notion of a blind person being able to hear light would have especially appealed to Jarry, as he believed that the human senses were inadequate to interpreting the 'other world' that existed around us.[29]

Confusingly there were two manuscripts of *Faustroll*. Known as the Lormel and the Fasquelle manuscripts, one was bought in 1907 by Louis Lormel, after Jarry had sold three of his manuscripts to raise some money;[30] the other was published by Eugène Fasquelle in 1911 after his death. Between writing the first and the second Jarry had changed his mind seven times about his most favoured books![31]

Faustroll cannot be described as a normal novel and Vallette turned it down for publication as a volume. Thadée Natanson also refused it. Superficially, it can seem a collection of disconnected chapters, only bound together by the thread of Faustroll's navigation. Each one demands to be read as an individual entity and requires detailed knowledge of the work of the dedicatee. 'To record a tiny part of the Beauty that he knew', was Faustroll's stated aim at the beginning of the book; 'to record a tiny part of the Truth that he had learned' was his second aim. The book could therefore be regarded as an important compendium of Jarry's personal philosophy.

In order to give this collection a narrative structure Jarry borrowed an idea from the Fifth Book of Rabelais, in which Pantagruel sails from island to island in search of the Holy Bottle. Each chapter or 'island' has a dedicatee. Whether writers, artists, scientists or musicians, most of his dedicatees are given the title of King or Master of their island. Not all the chapters of *Faustroll* take the form of tributes to their dedicatees. Some are colourful slanders as in the case of Louis Lormel, the writer Pierre Loti, and the unfortunate Christian Beck, cast as a baboon. In the case of Beardsley, Jarry's undoubted tribute to the artist's technical skill also alludes to a failure of artistic courage and a soul in anguish. He made a further moral declaration by including the public executioner among those to whom he paid homage. His dedication, *To Monsieur Deibler, sympathetically*, ensured that there should be no confusion about his intention.[32]

Most of Jarry's dedicatees were living writers and artists, known to the author, but he made no distinction between his regular contacts: Thadée Natanson, Alfred Vallette, Rachilde, Léon Bloy, Franc-Nohain, Gustave Kahn, Laurent Tailhade, Marcel Schwob, Claude Terrasse, Pierre Quillard, Paul Fort, Pierre Bonnard, André-Ferdinand Hérold and Félix Fénéon, and those whom he knew less well: Aubrey Beardsley, Émile Bernard, Paul Gauguin,

Stéphane Mallarmé, Henri de Régnier and Louis Dumur, co-founder of the *Mercure de France*. Paul Valéry, a fan both of Ubu and of Jarry's poetry, falls between the two categories.[33] Three of the chapters are dedicated to the British physicists C. V. Boys, Lord Kelvin and William Crookes, who were not personal friends, but whose scientific discoveries he put on the same imaginative level as the literary ones that he admired.

A mysterious chapter titled *Clinamen* and dedicated to his friend Paul Fort seems to describe thirteen as yet unidentified pictures, six with religious themes. The phenomenon of Clinamen, described by Lucretius, as a minute deviation or swerve that sometimes occurs in the normal vertical fall of atoms, had caught Jarry's imagination and became a central component of his pataphysical philosophy, to which an earlier chapter of *Faustroll* is entirely devoted. 'Pataphysics', writes Jarry, 'is the science of the particular . . . It will study the laws governing exceptions and will explain the universe supplementary to this one.'[34] In an unpublished fragment, that relates to his poem, 'Le Sablier', Jarry equated Clinamen to Chance:

All my hours are equal to each other, whether I am dreaming or awake. Let the order of the grains of sand be inverted and the rosary be broken.

The Clinamen of friendly hours collides with my sand, with which it agglutinates in its arbitrary fall. (Chance.)[35]

Clinamen's relevance to the chapter describing the thirteen pictures that follow is not clear, unless it refers to the arbitrary movement of the Painting Machine responsible for them. Jarry describes this movement as similar to that of a spinning top with its unpredictable darting and swaying trajectory. One would expect paintings in the style of Jackson Pollock to emanate from the several tubes of the spinning Painting Machine, described as colliding with walls and pillars. Yet Jarry's meticulous accounts of the thirteen pictures are far from abstract. They all depict recognizable characters, objects and landscapes, whose colours are carefully recorded. Red, blue and green predominate.

Several theories for the source of the *Clinamen* 'pictures' have been proposed, but no single theory is satisfactory.[36] It would be reasonable to assume that Fort, as dedicatee, would have known them. Given that he had a collection of old prints that he had put at Jarry's disposal for *L'Ymagier*, some of the descriptions could refer to hand-coloured popular engravings of his own. Jarry is so precise about the colours that they must relate to real pictures, some perhaps Épinal images:

> God is young and gentle with a pink halo. His robe is blue and his gestures curving. The Tree has twisted roots and slanting foliage. The other trees are not doing anything except being green. Adam is worshipping him and looking to see if Eve is too. They are on their knees.[37]

A black and white piece, *Fear makes silence*, seems to conjure up a macabre engraving with the atmosphere of Odilon Redon's *Closed Eyes*:

> There is nothing so frightening as a lone gallows, a bridge with dried up piers and shadows that are content just to be black. Fear turning her head away, keeps her eyelids lowered and the lips of her stone mask closed.[38]

It is possible that one day the key to the pictures of *Clinamen* may be found. Indeed the first piece, titled 'Nebuchadnezzar changed into a beast', takes the form of a vivid cinematic progression that seems to combine several engravings by William Blake. Jarry enjoyed the exercise of selecting distinctive pieces from the works of his chosen writers and artists and stringing them into a fictitious narrative of his own. Pure fantasy was difficult for him, but factual description also ran counter to his nature. The exercise of relating what he wrote to reality is therefore a fraught one.

Dr Faustroll, pataphysician, was the heir to Monsieur Ubu, pataphysician, but what is Jarry's pataphysics? The word 'pataphysics' was already current at the Lycée de Rennes. Monsieur Hébert's habitual term, 'science en physique', was transformed by the boys into 'science en pataphysique'. According to the myth that they built up around Hébert, he had been baptized with 'Essence of Pataphysics' endowing him with magical powers.[39] These pataphysical powers were what helped him in the heroic adventures that the boys constructed for him. Pataphysics was therefore not an invention of Jarry's, but a part of the Hébertique baggage that he took with him to Paris and gradually adapted. When Monsieur Ubu, newly transformed from Monsieur Ébé in *Guignol*, Jarry's first published piece, reveals himself to be 'a great Pataphysician', the word still carried a gloss of the ridiculous.[40] For *Ubu Roi* Jarry would go on to create a more human Ubu, whose vices and weaknesses were not reinforced by magical powers. Dr Faustroll, on the other hand, voyaging into worlds of the imagination, took on some of the characteristics of the earlier Ubu-magician.

After *Guignol*, Jarry's next move was to create apparent academic credentials for Pataphysics. By means of an ingenious footnote, he disassociates himself from its invention, implying that it was already an officially recognized term, described in encyclopædias or dictionaries. Not normally given to using the formal apparatus of academic texts, his allusive '(cf. *Pataph.*)' appears in the only footnote in the whole of his work. He inserts it into the extremely serious preface to *Les Minutes de Sable Mémorial*, where he instructs his potential readers into the approach they must take to his work. The footnote explains his use of the word 'simplicity', the definition of which had become a bone of contention between Gauguin and the critic, Alphonse Germain. 'Simplicity does not have to be simple', wrote

Jarry, 'but complexity, compressed and synthesized.'[41] In the summer of 1894, under the influence of Gauguin, Filiger and Seguin, Jarry thus decided to join the principles of Pataphysics to those of the new artistic movements of Cloisonnisme and Synthetism, also espoused by the Nabis. The fact that he later devoted the final page of what was to be the final number of his journal, *Perhinderion*, to reprinting an extract of the first article to coin the name Cloisonnisme and define its principles, deriving as they did from the economic style of Japanese prints, is symptomatic of his own identification with those principles:

> What is the point of recapturing the thousand insignificant details that the eye perceives? One must take hold of the essential feature . . . A silhouette is enough to express a physiognomy. The painter, ignoring photographs with or without retouching, will only seek to set down, in the fewest possible lines and characteristic colors, the intimate reality, the essence of the object that he commands . . . the brushstroke, almost abstract sign, gives the object its character.[42]

It is fitting that the author of this piece, Édouard Dujardin, walked side by side with Jarry in Mallarmé's funeral procession.[43] Jarry felt that the principles of the new style of painting could also be applied to the compressed style of polysemic writing honed by Mallarmé, whose severe economy was intellectually challenging to both writer and reader. From July 1894 the pataphysics of Rennes, which had been linked to Monsieur Hébert, changed its frivolous character and became an artistic and literary philosophy of which Jarry decided to take charge.

We have already seen one of Jarry's descriptions of pataphysics as the science that would study the laws governing exceptions. It forms a part of the preamble to the somewhat different formal definition of pataphysics given in Book II of *Faustroll*, which is titled 'Elements of Pataphysics'. The word 'DEFINITION' is written in upper case as if to isolate it from the rather confusingly verbose preamble. 'Pataphysics is the science of imaginary solutions, which symbolically attributes to the lineaments of objects the properties described by their virtuality.'[44] This 'definition' combines elements from two seemingly incompatible disciplines. On the one hand Jarry returns to the notion of Pataphysics that he conceived in 1894 in relation to Symbolist art, emphasizing the role of the lineament or contour as the sole unit of expression needed to express the 'essence' of an object; on the other he steps into abstract argument, the domain of philosophy, to define Pataphysics as 'the science of imaginary solutions'. His later article, 'Ce que c'est que les ténèbres' (On the nature of darkness) helps to explain what Jarry means by the second half of his definition. Here Jarry states that 'scientific imagination' is the only kind that he understands. In his lifetime the frontiers of science were being rapidly expanded. The recent discovery of x-rays had followed that of the other invisible forms of light, infrared and ultra-violet. Jarry was convinced that the human senses were inadequate to the task of perceiving all existing phenomena. He believed that our senses of hearing, smell and sight might not work in other worlds, but speculated whether a world of phenomena that we could not sense was not already around us.[45] 'Pataphysics', Jarry writes in the preamble to his definition, 'will explain the universe supplementary to our own'. He modifies this by suggesting the less ambitious target of describing 'the universe that we ought perhaps to see' in place of what he calls 'the traditional universe'. The laws that we believe we have discovered in this traditional universe, he views to be correlations of exceptions that just happen to be more frequent than the accidental ones. In his role as self-appointed definer and prophet of pataphysics, a concept that began life as a joke word, Jarry commits to constructing what looks like a serious doctrine but never forgets its nonsensical origins, and nor should we. He constructs an imaginary etymology for the word *'pataphysics* – *ἔπι (μετὰ τὰ φυσικὰ)* (*sic*, Jarry's own words) – explaining that an apostrophe should precede the opening *p*, if only to avoid the pun *patte à physique* (*physics paw*), and that it describes the realm of a science extending as far beyond metaphysics as metaphysics extends beyond physics.[46] Jarry therefore steps outside all accepted scientific laws and, under the heading of 'pataphysics, invites a latitude of scientific imagining which has no limits.

At the end of 1898 the supplementary universe lost some of its significance for Jarry when a very practical dilemma threatened his immediate world. There was a break-in at the Phalanstère and the neighbouring villa. The intruder, having fried himself some eggs in the kitchen, seems to have been disturbed by the arrival of the lady next door and, although clothes and letters from the Vallettes' drawers were strewn on the floor, nothing was taken. On 20 November Jarry informed Vallette that he had hammered a large nail into the broken door to make it secure. As this was the door through which he always accessed his own room and Vallette had the front door keys, he summoned a locksmith. He also summoned the cleaning lady to clear up the mess in the kitchen and the Vallettes' room. The locksmith made matters worse by breaking the lock. Vallette suspected that Jarry was responsible and sent a furious message. Jarry now wrote two lengthy letters, one to Rachilde and one to Vallette to explain his course of action. At the end of the latter Jarry gave in his notice and offered to pay what he owed in terms of rent and expenses.[47] The Vallettes refused his offer, but the owners of the Phalanstère had in any case decided to put the house up for sale. Its survival was threatened by plans for a new road. Jarry's peaceful solitary occupancy of the villa and his healthy outdoor existence, in which he could live by his fishing rod, was about to end.

8

Through the Dimensions

When in Paris, Jarry's routine was to work at the Bibliothèque Nationale during the day and to spend the evenings drinking. Rachilde accused his friends, who had wives and comfortable beds to go home to, of thoughtlessly encouraging him.[1] At Corbeil his existence was healthier. He would usually spend a couple of hours fishing – his letters variously mention ten o'clock to midday, midday to two o'clock or even dawn till eight o'clock. He was drinking too, but not as much as in later years.

Jarry was certainly finding time to write. Two projects were under way. The first was an *Almanach du Père Ubu*, a volume of 92 pages in small format, illustrated by Pierre Bonnard, who had now become Jarry's regular illustrator. His brother Charles undertook the publication and it went to print with Renaudie at the end of 1898. The second project would turn out to be literally gargantuan and he was never able to complete it. Jarry had agreed with Terrasse to write the libretto for a five-act *opéra bouffe, Pantagruel*, whose composition and constant revision, running to thousands of pages, would drag on for eight years. In Jarry's last will and testament, he stipulated that four twelfths of the proceeds of *Pantagruel* were due to him, as he had done the majority of the work on it. A deleted line states more emotionally that he had actually taken on the entire burden of the work, leading to the 'acute neurasthenia' from which he was dying.[2] Neurasthenia was a popular diagnosis at that time, relating to a wide range of what would now be regarded as stress induced illnesses.

Realizing that Jarry's heart was not in the *Pantagruel* project, Terrasse soon had recourse to summoning him to his house at Noisy-Le-Grand in the eastern suburbs of Paris and more or less imprisoning him in his room. This was also a way of ensuring that the impecunious writer got regular meals and did not drink more than was good for him. Later, to Jarry's discomfiture, the exile would be even further from Paris, at Terrasse's house at Grand-Lemps in the mountains north of Grenoble. Andrée, Terrasse's wife and the Bonnards' sister, had been accompanist for the Pantins and Jarry was almost regarded as one of the family. The Terrasse children adored Père Ubu, as did Gabrielle Vallette, but the role of 'uncle' in a comfortable family existence was not to Jarry's taste, nor did he take to the restrictions on his alcohol intake.

Despite the *Pantagruel* interruptions, Jarry had completed a new novel, *L'amour absolu*, before he was forced to vacate the Phalanstère at the end of February 1899. It concerned his own past, following the semi-autobiographical genre of *Les Jours et les Nuits* and had been preoccupying him more than the doggerel needed for *Pantagruel.* He had originally intended it as the final chapter of *L'Amour en Visites* where it had carried the title *Chez Dame Jocaste*. Anticipating Freud, he must have realized that he could bend the Oedipus theme to an imaginary treatment of his relationship with his own mother and father. In hanging the ancient myth on to a modern scientific framework, he used the latest psychological research into hysteria and hypnosis, mainly derived from experiments on women. Young writers often used to observe Dr Jean-Michel Charcot's experiments at the Salpétrière Hospital, but Charcot's publications, as well as the work of Pierre Janet on automatism and hysteria, and Pierre Azam on hypnotism would have given Jarry the material he needed.[3] He already believed in the associative power of the unconscious mind to create connections between words and to construct extraordinary combinations. For *L'amour absolu* he invented broken dialogues, based on the

Jarry at Claude Terrasse's house at Noisy-le-Grand, 1904.

results of Janet, who had reported the conversations that he had held with his female subjects while under deep hypnosis. It was an adventurous technique to try out in a novel.

Fearing rebuff, Jarry had avoided raising the subject of his novel with Vallette at a *mardi* of Rachilde's in the spring of 1898. His subsequent brusque letter, dated only 'Wednesday morning', is uncompromising:

> Comrade,
>
> I forgot to mention the subject of my octodecimo yesterday and this morning I got up far too late to come and tell you about it. Take it as read, that even if it seems to be unmarketable by the Mercure, I'm not prepared to change either the order of the chapters or indeed anything else.
>
> If, in the case of possible acceptance by the committee, the Mercure was not able to guarantee an honourable and rapid publication (by that I mean something like May) it would be completely pointless to go through the formal process of

submitting the aforementioned octodecimo to the committee
and I would ask for its return when I come to the Mercure
on Sunday.

Best wishes

A. Jarry[4]

In the event Jarry had fifty copies of *L'amour absolu* printed as a
facsimile manuscript, apparently out of his own pocket, although
the Mercure acted as the depository and it may well be that Vallette
came to his rescue privately.[5] There is a list of twenty people to
whom Jarry intended to send free copies, many deleted. The name
Melmoth, the pseudonym that Oscar Wilde adopted after his
release, remains undeleted, although that of Henry Davray, who
introduced them, is.[6] A letter from Jarry of October 1905 offering
the remaining 32 or 33 copies to a bookseller indicates that none
at all had been properly sold.[7]

The narrator of *L'amour absolu* is apparently a condemned man
awaiting execution for the murder of his mother, but the situation
is far from clear. At the end of the first chapter, we are told that if,
however, he has not killed, or *if it is not understood that he has killed*,
'he has no other prison than the box of his own skull and is simply
a man dreaming by his lamp'.[8] The reader is therefore left in doubt
as to whether the story that follows is merely the wild imagining
of a wandering mind, for the plot hinges on a burgeoning sexual
relationship between the narrator, as a fifteen-year-old schoolboy,
and his adoptive mother. A further confusion springs from the fact
that the story is interwoven with real episodes from Jarry's own
childhood, which include his first teacher, Madame Venel, and his
earliest schoolmates. This is not the only confusion – the criminal's
name is Emmanuel Dieu, apparently the Son of God, and his father
and mother bear the Breton equivalents of Joseph and Mary, Joseb
and Varia, as their names. Nor is Varia's identity constant. At one
moment she is Varia, a version not only of Jarry's own mother, but

of Eve, representing Jarry's view of woman as erotic, inconstant and deceitful; at the next she is Miriam, the Hebrew Mary, a holy figure, whose spirit survives beyond the grave. In her many-faceted identity she has been seen as the poetic sister of Joyce's Anna Livia Plurabelle.[9] 'Emmanuel Dieu knew', writes Jarry, 'that in *murdering* Varia, he had not killed Miriam! . . .The real Miriam was outside Varia.'[10] In his biography of Jarry, Beaumont suggests that by writing *L'Amour absolu* Jarry was attempting to expunge a lifelong sense of guilt that he was in some way responsible for the death of his mother, or at least had been the cause of the illness and exhaustion that had killed her.[11]

The final chapter of *L'Amour absolu* catches the flavour of the religious devotion that Caroline Jarry had passed to her son when he was a small boy. Emmanuel Dieu gazes at a granite statue of a Breton Virgin Mary and recaptures his childhood sensation that she is real and can move. The Sunday procession of Breton women, filing out of church like a fleet of sailing ships in their white coifs, disperses. They are instantly replaced by children emerging on the hillside to fly their kite, as he would have done himself. Even the kite rising into the sky, with its wooden frame in the shape of a cross, has religious significance for him. A sudden shower dashes the kite and brings a shutter down on this scene. *L'amour absolu* is the most personal of Jarry's novels and contains passages of real poetic beauty. It is no wonder that he did not want to change a single word.

Despite the fact that Vallette had rejected *L'amour absolu*, he was still open to publishing Jarry's more incidental work in the house journal. Jarry often wrote in different genres at the same time. Several of the *Faustroll* chapters had been devoted to scientific subjects. Inspired by H. G. Wells's *The Time Machine*, Jarry had sent Vallette a long, five-part article, *Commentary for Use in the Practical Construction of the Time Machine*. Whereas Wells's imagination had focused on the social and anthropological possibilities of the year 802,701 and to the way that a time traveller might interact with his future counterparts, Jarry's scientific mind, with its pataphysical slant, was drawn to the technicalities of how a time machine might work and how to construct one. In agreeing to the article, Vallette gently reminded him of his chief fault, which was to assume that his readers were as well versed in his subject as he was:

> Père Ubu must agree to be clear . . . In a *spoken* demonstration, it's always easier to understand him, because he takes longer over it than when writing. Sensing when he has not been fully understood, he explains and anyway one can always ask questions. But in a *written* demonstration, he wrongly assumes that certain things are known and not worth explaining, when either they are not known, or have slipped the mind, because not mentioned [earlier] in the demonstration.
> Tell him this, and that I'll need his article by the 13th or 14th.[12]

Jarry did indeed make an effort to be clear in his exposé, which proposes a definition of Time either as a fourth dimension of Space or as an essentially different locus, defined as containing events, as opposed to physical bodies. He suggests that both Space and Time may be different forms of motion or even of thought. His belief that it is possible to slip from one part of time into another is integral to the structure of *L'amour absolu* and of *Messaline,* his next novel. His argument is simple enough to follow when he states that Space is usually considered to be solid, whereas the standard poetic image of Time is a liquid stream moving in a straight line. His reasoning becomes more abstruse, however, when he asserts, in the same sentence, that the stream of Time consists of mobile molecules, whose slippage or viscosity actually represents human consciousness. Here he leapfrogs all the steps that lead to this conclusion.

Jarry envisaged the interior of the Time Machine as protected from the passing of Time. It would therefore be possible, he speculated, to be isolated from the ageing process by locking oneself in and achieving a stationary transparent state whereby events simply passed through one, leaving no mark. Immobile in Space while Time continued passing, he foresaw the possibility of exploring all past and future instants from a static viewpoint within the machine. The article is one of his most thoughtful and serious pieces, drawing heavily on the lectures and publications of William Thomson, Lord Kelvin, which he cites. Yet, by signing it in the name of Dr Faustroll rather than his own, Jarry placed the article firmly in the realm of the imaginary. When *Les Gestes et opinions du docteur Faustroll, pataphysicien* was finally published by Fasquelle in 1911, four years after Jarry's death, it was appropriately placed as the final chapter of the book, following the other scientific chapters: Faustroll's two 'telepathic letters' to Lord Kelvin and his complex mathematical instructions on how to measure the surface of God.

The year of 1899, however, saw Jarry at the age of 26, making hardly any money at all from his writing. At the same time he had been forced to leave Corbeil and return to the less salubrious conditions of the last and smallest of his Paris dwellings. Having taken on the tiny apartment at 7 rue Cassette when he had moved out of Rousseau's lodgings at the end of 1897, he had hardly used it, except to keep his books and papers. The owner of this building had calculated that he could get an extra rent out of it by cutting the third floor in half. Jarry's small stature especially qualified him for the consequent low ceiling, but even he acquired a permanent sprinkling of plaster flakes in his hair and wrote stretched out on a thin pine wood board.[13]

Jarry glamourized all his dwellings with special names. This one became 'Notre Grande Chasublerie' by virtue of its proximity to a manufacturer of ecclesiastical vestments on the floor below him. His strange address, the second and half floor, also lent an air

Rachilde in Jarry's trailer with Vallette at La Frette, 1899.

of mystery to his very basic living conditions. His fame through *Ubu Roi* drew talented young writers to pay him court and it is due to the observations of Apollinaire and Max Jacob that detailed descriptions of the Grande Chasublerie exist.

Jarry's reduced circumstances in the rue Cassette, by comparison with his boulevard Saint-Germain apartment, did not deter him from inviting Claudius-Jacquet, his friend from the Lycée Henri IV, but his extreme willingness to fit in with the younger man's arrangements shows no greater confidence that he would accept his invitation than three years previously. His urgent telegram of 23 March 1899 seems to refer to an earlier conversation and implies that Jarry had changed his plans:

My dear Claudius,

All in all, I've decided to stay at home today. It would give me great pleasure if you can come as soon as convenient for you.

We'll have dinner, of course. In case my telegram gets to you too late, I won't be going out either tonight, or tomorrow afternoon.

Affectionately,

Alfred Jarry[14]

Although three years apart, both Jarry's surviving letters to Claudius-Jacquet offer his friend alternative opportunities to meet. As an enticement, Jarry is at pains to reassure him that dinner will be included in the programme, something that he might well have had reason to doubt. Jarry's two letters betray an uncharacteristic lack of self-confidence. Although he attempted to pick up his former friendship with the younger man after his absence in Corbeil, Jarry remained fearful of destroying it. It was a fear he had already fictionalized in *Les Jours et les Nuits.* Unfortunately the outcome of his invitations and the path of the friendship itself remain as uncharted as the rest of Jarry's intimate life. Jacquet's name appears as the fiftieth and final beneficiary on his list of complimentary copies for *L'Amour en Visites* of 1898. It is absent from the list of Jarry's twenty closest literary friends who received the privately printed *L'amour absolu* of 1899.

Jarry's return to Paris did not last long. As soon winter was over, he set about looking for a new riverside villa to replace the Phalanstère and took charge of the arrangements. By mid-May he had completed a deal on behalf of the Vallettes to rent a house on the Seine, north-west of Paris at La Frette-Montigny. Unfortunately he had failed to notice its proximity to a large sewage farm, whose outflow had not only killed the local fish but whose fumes, as the weather became warmer, became rapidly unbearable to Rachilde. Cycling trips replaced the canoeing. Jarry constructed a trailer for Rachilde on the back of his bicycle. She recounts how Jarry drew a knife to cut her loose as they were hurtling, out of control, towards a viaduct one day, but that, at the last minute, he flung himself and the bicycle to the ground. 'Never have we wanted to take leave of a woman so badly', he announced. With torn trousers he reported that nothing was broken except his left pedal. He made no distinction, writes Rachilde, between his own bones and his bicycle frame.[15]

After July there is a hiatus in Jarry's known correspondence. He stayed on alone at the villa, writing and largely out of contact with the rest of the world. It was here that he completed both *Ubu Cocu* and *Ubu enchaîné*, the latter conceived as the obverse of *Ubu*. In *Ubu Enchaîné*, when Ubu steps on to the stage, he says nothing. Mère Ubu asks him whether he has forgotten the Word and he replies that it has got him into too much trouble. Of his own volition Ubu becomes a slave and wants nothing better than to serve and to receive lashes for his pains. The Palotins are replaced by the Free Men, whose mission to disobey every order is just as irksome as obeying. The play would not be produced until 1937 when the Surrealist movement was at its height. Max Ernst, who was fascinated by the figure of Ubu, created the set.

Jarry had not been idle in the first half of 1900. Based in Paris during this period, he had the Bibliothèque Nationale once more within easy reach. He took full advantage of this to research his next novel. Possibly hoping to emulate the success of Pierre Louÿs' best-selling erotic novel, *Aphrodite*, he took the life of the prostitute empress, Messalina, wife of the Emperor Claudius, as his subject. Louÿs and Jarry shared a profound knowledge of Greek and Latin literature. Signs of their friendship are obvious from references to Jarry in Louÿs' correspondence with Tinan and Valéry. Jarry had attended Louÿs' wedding in June 1899. It is also significant that Louÿs bought one of the two *Messaline* manuscripts at a 1918 auction.[16] The full title of the novel was *Messaline, roman de l'ancienne Rome*, soon to be followed by its pendant, *Le Surmâle, roman moderne.* Jarry researched the ancient sources meticulously and cites them at the head of each chapter, but for all the authentic period detail that he provides, the picture that he paints of decadent Rome parallels the more florid aspects of the landscape and culture that surrounded him in Paris. In *Messaline* the gardens of Versailles and Lalique's vases each have their Roman equivalents. It is possible that Jarry's rural existence and his impoverished state led him to view the excesses of high society with an even more critical eye. His satirical instincts were certainly to the fore.

Five years after warning readers that he would be playing Blind Man's Buff with them in *Les Minutes de Sable Mémorial*, it is difficult to ascertain whether Jarry has disguised living people including himself in *Messaline*. The main plot follows the insatiable empress from her sessions in the filthy Roman brothels to her execution, where she greets the hard steel of the centurion's sword piercing her throat as if it were the sacred Phallus for which she has been searching. The novel's sub-plot concerns Mnester, the leading acrobat and dancer of his era, whom Messaline fails to seduce. Jarry describes Mnester as sexually cold, linking him to his own extreme misogyny. In his version of the story he exaggerates and prolongs the period that Mnester is supposed to have felt repulsion for Messalina. Suetonius records that they sleep together but in Jarry's version, after drinking an infusion of absinthe that acts as a diuretic, Mnester urinates into the empress instead of coming to a sexual climax.[17] In revenge, she persuades Claudius to have him executed.

It is not too far fetched to see elements of Remy de Gourmont in the person of the Emperor Claudius, disfigured by a scar on his face, similar to the critic's facial blemish. Berthe de Courrière already had the reputation of a Messalina! Mère Ubu may not have had Messalina's sexual appetites but her manipulation of Ubu echoes Messalina's manipulation of Claudius and Courrière's of Gourmont. Jarry regarded treachery, infidelity and deceit as intrinsically female characteristics. Only the Virgin Mary was excepted.

At one level, the novel is a deeply sardonic account not only of betrayal, but a depiction of the communication barrier between the artist and the general public. Mnester is ordered by Claudius to perform a dance in the arena for his birthday. Like a gladiator, he faces the whistles and catcalls of the Roman public when he begins his performance with a phase of motionless meditation that bores them.[18] The central, climactic chapter of the novel describes the dangerous acrobatic dance that Mnester performs. This involves a daredevil somersault of one and half turns in the air. An error of timing would have meant breaking his neck, which lends the act its excitement. But Mnester's daring is not so much physical as political, for he also sings a forbidden song. In singing himself, rather than dancing to the words of a choir, he not only broke with Roman custom, Jarry writes, but infringed Claudius's law forbidding mention of the name of Caligula.[19] The song should actually have been in honour of Claudius, but Mnester had been Caligula's lover and he sings in honour of his late master instead.

There are signs within the text that Jarry used this chapter whose theme was a tribute to a male lover, to incorporate private allusions to Wilde and to 'the Love that dare not speak its name'. For example, the odd comparison of the sound of Mnester's song to the 'death rattle of a *wild* beast' (*râle de fauve*) suggests Wilde's surname.[20] Mnester's song to Caligula would then take on the double role of a 'forbidden' eulogy in both the ancient and the modern context. As a satirist, that was something that Jarry would have found supremely satisfying. The homage, if homage it is, would be at a very private level.

For Jarry to link Wilde with a Roman emperor would not be surprising. During his earlier sojourn in Paris of 1883, Wilde had deliberately cultivated a Roman appearance and sported a hairstyle modelled on a bust at the Louvre that he took his hairdresser to visit.[21] He also had his portrait painted in this mode. The case for a secret homage to Wilde by Jarry would be stronger if *Messaline* had been completed after Wilde's death on 30 November 1900. *Messaline* was serialized in *La Revue blanche* between July and

September 1900. Wilde became ill during the summer, but did not contract the ear infection that killed him until early autumn. On the other hand, Jarry would have been able to have the relevant numbers of *La Revue blanche* sent to him and, as he wrote, at least had the pleasure of knowing that Wilde might read his novel.

With *Messaline* Jarry anticipated a shift in public taste, to which Diaghilev's exotic productions would play so successfully. The novel is a pioneer work in French dance literature, celebrating a male dancer at a time when male dancers were only accepted in supporting roles. Jarry's portrayal of the Roman dancer Mnester

Oscar Wilde with 'Neronic' hairstyle, photographed by Napoleon Sarony in 1883.

looked forward rather than back, responding to the growing popularity and sophistication of circus performances. The magnificent spectacles provided by Barnum's and the Nouveau Cirque would inspire two of his most thoughtful articles.[22] The circus had been drawing middle class audiences away from the theatre, ballet and concert hall for some time. Unfortunately Jarry would not live to experience the rapturous reception of the Ballets Russes in 1909 and in 1911 of Nijinsky, who combined what had been considered the 'low' art of acrobatics with the 'high' art of dance.

Messaline is a complex novel that charts Jarry's belief in a fourth dimension and the pataphysical possiblility of switching between past and present space and time. Through its serialisation in *La Revue blanche* journal, it reached a much larger audience than any other of Jarry's novels. Félix Fénéon, *La Revue blanche*'s éminence grise, who had encouraged Jarry since his earliest reviewing days, used his influence to secure him a regular slot in the journal. Simultaneously with the publication of the first instalment of *Messaline* in July 1900, Jarry began to contribute book reviews. At last he was earning a regular income. The satirical tone of *La Revue blanche* with its anarchistic sympathies was also much more suited to his outlook than the *Mercure de France.* Under the aegis of *La Revue blanche* he would develop a much simpler, more readable style. He would soon put this to good effect in *Le Surmâle*, the last novel that he would be able to complete. Jarry had not yet exhausted his very twentieth-century preoccupation with exploring the limits of human athletic and sexual prowess, and his skill as a writer was also acquiring a new sharpness.

9

Journalism, *Le Surmâle* and Brussels

Jarry was very comfortable with his new role of book reviewer for *La Revue blanche*. Fénéon gave him a free hand to choose which books he reviewed, whether fishing manuals or the latest translation of *One Thousand and One Nights*. It is obvious from the *Almanach du Père Ubu* and from *Messaline* that he was already an astute observer and critic of the contemporary social scene and he was soon allowed to graduate to writing pieces of social commentary. His observations are sharp, funny and ironic; many remain extraordinarily pertinent to the problems of society today. The concise format of an article suited him perfectly. Because he was now writing for the general reader, he was also forced to express himself simply and clearly. His journalism represents quite a different brand of literature to any of his earlier writing and raises his stature.

With his entrée to *La Revue blanche* secured in the summer of 1900, Jarry could plan a period of relative financial security. Hearing that the Vallettes had managed to rent the first floor of a house upstream from Corbeil, he moved swiftly to rent a riverside dwelling of his own nearby. Hardly deserving the designation of *chaumière* or 'thatched cottage' given it by Rachilde, it was really an old stable that had previously been used to rear rabbits.[1] Located close to the Coudray Weir, Jarry's new refuge was in happy proximity to a fishermen's bar called the 'Rendez-vous du Barrage', to whose owners, the Dunous, it belonged. Jarry divided his drinking time between this bar and another owned by Mère Fontaine, a former

Son château et ses … remises.

Jarry's Coudray shack, early 1900s.

lady of the night. Both she and Madame Dunou had a soft spot
for Jarry and constantly wiped what he owed off the slate. His
beloved summer routine of fishing and canoeing with Vallette,
and then repairing to a bar either with the locals or his stout friend,
Demolder, was once again feasible. His domestic arrangements
were far less comfortable than before, however, and Rachilde,
although she complimented the colourful avant-garde posters
on his walls, wrote with horror about the detritus of fishbones
and leaves on the earthen floor. On the other hand, Jarry had
complete privacy, whereas at the Phalanstère he could only access
his own bedroom through a trapdoor in the Vallettes' bedroom
floor. Jarry haughtily declined Rachilde's offer to send him her
cleaner, retorting that the wind (*celui qui souffle*) was his sweeper.[2]

Between 1 July 1900 and 15 April 1903 Jarry reviewed 72 separate
books. His selection is very eclectic, but he took advantage of his
column to give positive reviews to books written or illustrated by
his friends, particularly Rachilde, Mirbeau, Demolder, Bonnard and
Louise France. It is in his mature reviews in *La Plume* of 1903 that
his application of contemporary scientific discoveries to literary
commentary is at its most accomplished. His article on Rachilde's
La Princesse de ténèbres, titled 'Ce que c'est que les ténèbres', is less
a review than a speculation on the nature of darkness and on the
existence of other worlds where the human sense organs, adapted
as they are to this world, would be useless. With his early interest
in nocturnal creatures and night sight Jarry had never accepted
darkness as an impenetrable element. He portrays Rachilde as
enveloped in violet, the colour of the *Mercure de France*, evoking
the recently named ultra-violet rays, invisible to the human eye.
He cites Wells as among the science fiction writers who had tried
to imagine what other worlds would be like if one could reach
them. But what, speculates Jarry, if we are already in another world
that we cannot perceive?[3] In this and many other articles he placed
his observations on literature against a backcloth relating to

scientific discoveries or speculation that had tickled his curiosity or appealed to his sense of the absurd.

Without doubt Jarry's skill as a journalist improved with practice. It was his misfortune that, despite a successful life span of nine years, *La Revue blanche* was already in financial difficulties when he joined it, and that his happy association with it would only last until its demise in April 1903. By this time Jarry was at the height of his powers. In January 1903 he started contributing to *La Plume*. Some of his most polished articles date from this year, shared between *La Plume* and *Le canard sauvage*. One of his most original is 'La Passion considérée comme course de côte' ('The Passion considered as an uphill bicycle race'),[4] written for *Le Canard sauvage*. He removes this central tenet of the Christian faith from its religious context and places it in a modern sporting one, stripping it of all its usual sacred connotations. Christ's Passion, the Stations of the Cross, and the ascent of Mount Golgotha become a bicycle race, and Christ himself no more than an ordinary competitor who suffers an unfortunate accident.

The Via Dolorosa is a route with fourteen bends; Barabbas, on being freed, is immediately disqualified; Pilate is the referee responsible for starting and timing the race with a water-clock; St Matthew's record of Christ's flagellation is cited by Jarry in terms of a beneficial stimulant, normally administered to the contestants in advance of a race. Christ's cross is his bicycle, in front of which a spiteful saboteur scatters thorns, causing an instant puncture to the front tyre. Undeterred, the Saviour hoists it onto his back to pursue his course. Jarry goes on to cite what he calls the 'cyclophile hagiographers' who claim that the cross was equipped with a device called a *suppedaneum.* No need to be a great scholar, he writes, to identify this device as a 'pedal'. Jesus took his first tumble at the third turn, alarming his mother who was in the stands. His trainer, Simon of Cyrene, who, but for the thorn accident, would have been riding out in front to cut the wind, then takes over carrying the machine. With pedantic precision, Jarry reports Christ's excessive perspiration, in view of the fact that he was carrying nothing. Although it is not certain whether a female spectator wiped his brow, he writes, it is known that a reporter called Veronica obtained a photograph of him on her Kodak camera. Jarry records Jesus falling a second and a third time and finally 'the deplorable accident familiar to us all', which took place on the twelfth bend when he was 'in a dead heat with the two thieves'. Still maintaining his pedantic manner, he declines to elucidate the strange fact that Jesus decided to complete the course by air, as it falls outside his subject, he apologetically concludes. This irreverent interpretation of the Passion as a sporting event is an extraordinarily modern piece of satirical journalism, which would not have been out of place in performance in *Monty Python's Flying Circus.*

La Revue blanche was published fortnightly. The requirement to produce at least one article every two weeks held Jarry to a regular writing routine. In 1901 he was delivering copy by hand to the *La Revue blanche*'s offices at 1 rue Laffitte, which meant cycling into Paris from Coudray much more often. By 1902 he was pacing himself better and his letters show him relying more on the post.[5] During the period between 15 January 1901 and 15 December 1902 he sometimes wrote as many as five articles in a fortnight. The sum of his two series of articles (*Spéculations* and *Gestes*) reached a creditable total of 86 during that time. The position of *chroniqueur*, or commentator on social mores and current events, was not only respected, but well paid, allowing him to earn his living by his pen for a full two years and even to be invited to lecture. Unfortunately this happy state of affairs came to an abrupt end.

Jarry's journalism still appears so topical because his curiosity fastened on recently invented items of modern life, integral to the mechanics of society today: postage stamps; national flags; the camera; buses and bicycles. He even envisaged things that had not yet been invented such as moving walkways and cordless telephones. He would often adopt a peculiar perspective on a familiar object. He liked to take the point of view of a naturalist describing the habits of a strange species: shuttlecocks became birds, captured in nets;[6] the corpses of suicide victims floating past him in the Seine gruesomely became a species of fish;[7] buses were transformed into unusual pachyderms left over from the Stone Age.[8]

In his lecture *Le Temps dans l'art,* given to the Société des Artistes Indépendants in April 1902, Jarry argued that it was inappropriate for artists to aspire to exact historical reconstitution. He argued that ancient items all had their equivalents in the modern world. As an example, he equated the extreme frustration that we experience when we miss a bus to that experienced by our Stone Age ancestors when their prey got away, comparing the bus shelter to an ancient hunter's hide. On the frequent occasions when the bus was full, it would hoot as it approached, 'utter a raucous cry', in Jarry's description, and 'take flight', leaving those who had been so anxiously waiting for it gazing at the illuminated 'full' sign on its departing rear.[9]

Turning to the harsher scenario of behaviour in war, Jarry denied any lessening in the brutality of ancient practice. Once again he used the paradigm of sport. 'It is one of soldiery's favourite sports', he wrote, 'to use babies on their mothers' breasts for target practice and to try to dislodge them with a shot. The marksman would be disqualified – it goes without saying – if the bullet touched the mother, which goes to show that old fashioned French gallantry is still alive and well in the army.' In another article, 'Communication d'un militaire', he was equally scathing about French brutality in China following the Boxer Rebellion. Pursuing his earlier metaphor of floating corpses as a species of fish, he sarcastically recommended French soldiers to the Society for the Protection of Animals for not removing this Chinese species from their watery element and even for attempting to increase their numbers.[10]

Jarry sometimes pretended to adopt the pernickety moral attitude of an elderly lady. On the occasion of a new issue of more expensive stamps in January 1901 he turned his attention to how the postal service operates in France. He described the citizen's action of posting a letter when he wanted to communicate with absent loved ones as 'the superstitious practice of casting affectionate messages into apertures resembling drain holes'. In order to ensure the arrival of these messages, he observed, we buy little pictures, probably holy, which we kiss on the back. For some reason, he complained, these transactions have to be conducted at a tobacconist, despite the noxious effects of tobacco. In vain had he appealed to the stall-keeper's sense of morality as to the picture printed on the new stamp. The picture depicted France, the Republic, holding a notice proclaiming 'The Rights of Man'. Jarry pretended to interpret it as a blind woman, arm in sling, pathetically appealing to passers-by with a notice 'promising men every right upon her person'. Above her head, he noted, hung a lantern carrying the number of her house and observed that the price increased for foreigners, despite being the same woman. Giving citizens a completely impractical piece of advice that would obliterate the whole address, he counselled them to use instead as many of the 1, 2 or 5 centime stamps as necessary, with its more appropriate (in his view) picture of a winged horseshoe.[11]

Constantly challenging 'civilized' morals and conventional laws, Jarry would often take the side of the persecuted and the vulnerable. In his article, 'Paris colonie nègre', he put himself in the position of an inhabitant of the African jungles encountering northern European customs for the first time. On reading that the chief of police was urgently seeking a negro who had failed to pay for a large quantity of drinks and headbutted a waiter, Jarry compared his behaviour to that of the great European explorers. Was the negro not sampling the local products in the interests of African science, he suggests. And was the head butt not a form of *salaam*? Had he not been interrupted, Jarry speculated, he would no doubt have gone on to plant a few flags, burn some monuments and take various people into slavery.[12] Through his technique of transposing what might be considered 'normal' behaviour to an alien context, or by comparing it to 'bad' behaviour in a familiar context Jarry was better able to question its absolute morality. It was the closest that he came to making a political statement.

Jarry's two groups of articles for *La Revue blanche* in 1901 and 1902 came under the heading of *Spéculations* and *Gestes* or 'Exploits' respectively. In the *Spéculations*, he always adopts an opposite perspective to the norm, a technique that Mallarmé had practised to entertain his *mardi* guests, and one to which his young listener may well have been attentive. André Fontainas recalled listening to Mallarmé proposing a little fable about the workings of a ship's propeller (a feminine noun in French), one evening in February 1895. The poet insisted that, contrary to appearances, a propeller was not capable of pushing a ship by itself. Despite the gracefulness of its revolutions, he maintained, a ship would not be able to move by virtue of these alone. It only departs, said Mallarmé, when the water, attracted by the propeller's graceful seductive movements, approaches, flows into it, and, falling for the beautiful dancer's lures, pushes the ship and carries it along.[13]

Jarry's fictitious machines, nearly all female, were more vicious. The phonograph, subject of an early prose poem, is a metal siren that grips her beloved's head in her teeth.[14] It would appear again in his novel *Le Surmâle* as one of several pernicious machines, culminating in the Love-inspiring Machine. This was a fictionalized form of the American electric chair, whose current unexpectedly goes into reverse, causing the machine itself to fall in love with the Supermale and overheat. The platinum band fastened to his head becomes white hot, literally biting into his skull.[15] Jarry had based his account on newspaper reports of the first execution by electric chair in 1890, which had failed to kill its subject, William Kemmler, outright, searing the skin under the electrodes while he was still alive. The new machines, for Jarry, were simply an extension of predatory women, not new as a breed themselves, but whom he feared and avoided. Only the Painting Machine of *Faustroll*, with its powers of ejaculation, and a modern version of the ancient fertility totem of the sacred Phallus, escapes the trope of the machine as *femme fatale*.

Shortly before his death, when his income from writing had all but dried up, Jarry hoped to publish a collection of his best articles and compiled a plan of the titles of most of his *Spéculations* and *Gestes*. Of the 77 that he first selected, he drew up a smaller quantity to be published by Sansot under the title *Siloques, superloques, soliloques et interloques de Pataphysique*. When this project failed, he decided on a much broader selection of articles, to be called *La Chandelle verte, lumières sur les choses de ce temps*, which would include his later articles from *La Plume* and other journals. The plan never came to fruition, and it was not until 1969 that a complete collection of all Jarry's articles and book reviews was published by Maurice Saillet under his chosen title, *La Chandelle verte*. The Green Candle, the mysterious totem by which Père Ubu constantly swears, dates from the earliest Hébertique playlets conceived at Rennes. In these it used to be lit in the fictitious Père Eb's window as a signal to his accomplices. As such it acquired a near-magical status, signifying the start of a new adventure. The fact that Jarry's *chroniques* were placed under the sign of this imaginary beacon, which no doubt emitted a weird, greenish glow, appropriately reflects the author's oblique, not to say pataphysical approach.

As a journalist, Jarry's style is abrasive and often deeply ironic. He forces the reader to look at familiar objects in an unaccustomed light and makes many of the rules and laws governing French life sound ridiculous, throwing their basic morality into doubt. Why, he enquires, is the bounty for pulling a dead body out of the Seine ten centimes more than for rescuing a live person? Is this not an incentive to throw it back like an undersized fish and wait until its value had increased?[16] In another article he reports a young prostitute receiving a jail sentence for theft with tears of joy. Her gratitude was due to the fact that the completion of two jail sentences entitled prostitutes to an official permit allowing them to solicit legally, so converting their criminal status to one of respectability. Jarry's highly logical mind was finely tuned to inconsistencies such as these and the issues that he confronted were often deadly serious.

When he transferred to *La Plume* in 1903, Jarry reverted to literary matters. His column, *Le périple de la littérature et de l'art*, ran for exactly a year. A couple of his articles give a fascinating insight into his own creative processes and, in particular, on his involuntary plagiaristic tendencies. In an article on Georges D'Esparbes's *Petit Louis*, Jarry compares passages from this novel with similar passages from Rudyard Kipling's 'Toomai of the Elephants' from *The Jungle Book*. Rather than accusing D'Esparbes of imitating Kipling, he credits him with a masterly feat of transposition. Jarry explains that a literary masterpiece can act on the brain like a sports coach, triggering a series of associative ideas. He proposes that a really original brain functions like the stomach of an ostrich, in that it can digest anything, whether pebbles or pieces of iron, but claims that this mental process is entirely unconscious. He goes on to say that if an organ's action needed conscious effort on the part of its owner, it would mean that it could not work by itself, a very bad thing in the case of a writer's brain. It would be better for the writer to stop writing.[17]

Although Jarry insisted that the process he described was one of transposition rather than assimilation, his editor, Alfred Vallette, did not agree. In his obituary of Jarry, he credited him with great intelligence and originality, but called him an assimilator to the point of imitation.[18] Vallette could not help but be exasperated with the young writer, whom he described as both charming and unbearable, and who had become so much a part of his private life, but whom it became more and more difficult for him to help professionally.

1902 was a prolific year for Jarry, but marked the watershed of his writing career. In conjunction with his *Spéculations* he had been writing *Le Surmâle*, the last novel that he would complete. In *Le Surmâle* he returns to the question of sexual insatiability, for which Messalina had been made notorious through Juvenal's verse:

> *. . . Tamen ultima cellam*
> *Clausit, adhuc ardens rigidae tentigine vulvae,*
> *[Et lassata viris nec dum satiata recessit.]*

This sentence refers to the fact that the empress had been the last to close her cell in the so-called House of Happiness. Although tired from receiving men all night long, she was still consumed with lust and her vulva was still rigid, wrote Juvenal. Through his fictitious character, André Marcueil, the Supermale, Jarry discusses the possibility of a man being able to sustain equal heights of sexual performance, since the organs of both sexes are supposedly made up of the same elements.[19] As so often, Rabelais was his source. Rabelais had cited an astounding nugget mentioned in Pliny's *Natural History* and Theophrastus of Eresus' *History of Plants,* that, with the aid of a certain herb, an Indian had been able to achieve orgasm more than three score and ten times in succession. At a dinner with his American friends William Elson and Arthur Gough, Marcueil argues that this feat is perfectly possible. Listening to him, Elson's daughter, Ellen, is intrigued by the notion and whispers in his ear that she believes him. The reader is thus prepared at an early stage in the novel for what is going to take place.

Le Surmâle tells the story of two record-breaking achievements: one sporting and one sexual. Its subtitle, *roman moderne*, is well deserved. Jarry was one of the first novelists to celebrate the coming cult of the athlete that would dominate the twentieth century. Many of his articles are devoted to feats of athleticism, daring and speed, and it is hardly surprising that he would make this the theme of his final novel, pitting humans against the machines that, with their indefinitely repeating movement, were supposed to outperform and outlast them. The sporting feat narrated in *Le Surmâle* is a race between a five-man American cycling team and a train. Jarry himself used to enjoy racing against trains, and his hero, André Marcueil, participates as a single and secret racer, keeping pace alongside the carriage bearing the frail Ellen Elson. Believing Theophrastus' record of the Indian's feat, Elson determines to partner Marcueil in an attempt to surpass it.

Although *Le Surmâle* was not published by *La Revue blanche* until May 1902, Jarry dated the finished manuscript 18 December 1901. His account of the five-man bicycle race is gripping, and he clearly enjoyed putting his imagination to the technicalities of the long-distance cycle racing of the future. He anticipates the concentrated superfoods of future arctic exploration and space travel, for the team is nourished by the colourless, crumbly and bitter-tasting tablets of 'Perpetual Motion Food' invented by William Elson. Elson is also the inventor of the Love-inspiring Machine and a parodic version of Edison. Jarry's *roman moderne* focuses on the way that humans were beginning to take on the characteristics of machines, narrowing the gap between them. He reduces the act of making love to the level of a mechanical action. The cynical first line of the novel sets the tone: The act of love is of no importance, since it can be performed indefinitely.[20]

In *Le Surmâle* Jarry writes that during the last few years of the nineteenth century five- and six-man bicycle teams had beaten express trains over a distance of one or two miles. What they had never done was to sustain this feat over long distances. The incredible Ten-Thousand-Mile Race, or Perpetual Motion Food Race, is placed in the year 1920. The account of the race takes the form of a long report, supposedly written by one of the team for the *New York Herald*. The five cyclists' legs are shackled to their pedals with aluminium rods. Tightly strapped to their machine and bent with their heads lower than their saddles, they are at first towed along the prepared track running next to the railway line to initiate their momentum. The extraordinary climax of the race is reached when the fourth man dies and begins to decompose in the saddle. Pedalling against his rigor mortis, the team succeeds in breaking it to the extent that the inanimate skeleton takes on a furious momentum of its own. They pull ahead of the train and even leave the ground, but become aware of a strange shadow following them. This is the Supermale, who shortly appears ahead of them, cycling in front of the train itself. To Ted Oxborrow, the narrator, whom Jarry borrowed from real life, the figure at first appears bizarrely dressed in a topcoat and grey top hat, and is riding a heavy antiquated machine with solid rubber tyres and iron mudguards, but this illusion passes to reveal a cyclist with wild flowing locks, whose bulging muscles have split his shorts and whose racing bicycle has microscopic, super-efficient tyres.

The whole account of the race wavers between the real and the surreal. We know that reality has been left behind when a host of red roses that Marcueil had ordered his gardener to cut after an earlier conversation in his garden with Ellen Elson, magically reappear, glued to her carriage window. She, her father and Gough are actually travelling in the train against which the team are competing. From here she is also able to observe the progress of the mystery solo cyclist. Each day, as their petals fall off, the strange roses are replaced. Of its own volition, a bunch arrives at the winning post ahead of the competitors and is there to greet them at the end of the race. The mystery cyclist is, however, never seen again.

Into this surreal scenario, and before he embarks on his narration of the sexual marathon, Jarry now introduces a sinister note. A policeman arrives to announce that the body of a little girl has been found in the grounds of Marcueil's château. The date of her death happens to be the day of Marcueil's departure six days previously. Jarry insists on the detail that she was apparently raped to death, rather than killed after being raped. He leaves it open for the reader to decide whether the perpetrator of this act could have been

Marcueil or the magistrate who happened to find her. Marcueil casually remarks that there were similar cases along the route of the train journey from which he has just returned. The story that has so far appeared to be an amusing fantasy takes on a macabre colouring with the possibility that Marcueil could be criminal, if not bestial.

Marcueil now sets up the sexual competition to beat the legendary Indian. He recruits the character Dr Bathybius as the referee who will take the tally of the acts of copulation. Seven beautiful prostitutes are engaged to give the present-day 'Indian', who has not yet made an appearance, the best chance of beating his predecessor's record. Marcueil excuses himself and an unseen hand locks the prostitutes in. The hand belongs to Ellen Elson who wants to take on the entire challenge by herself. Marcueil reappears for dinner disguised as a Red Indian, naked, but picturesquely equipped with bearskin, peace pipe, moccasins and tomahawk.

At midnight, shut away on their own, the couple begin their attempt to attain and surpass the target of 80 acts of copulation in 24 hours in the spirit of a sporting match. Jarry's description of their first noisy embrace evokes the impact of two wrestlers engaging. After the figure 82 has been reached, Ellen loses consciousness, apparently killed by her ordeal. For the first time Marcueil shows an interest in her now prostrate body. He composes a poem, but the subject of the erotic verses that he recites as he drifts off to sleep does not seem to be Ellen and is not necessarily female at all.

Marcueil's poem is simply addressed to 'une forme', a feminine noun applicable to both sexes, and not 'une femme'. Similar linguistic tricks were used by Rimbaud when he wanted to disguise the gender of the subject of his poems. Chanted in a state of reverie, the poem evokes a tender act of love with none of the confrontational and competitive aspects of the previous 82 undertaken in the name of Marcueil's wager. Its erotic tone simply does not fit in with the previous narrative. Might Jarry, normally so secretive about his private feelings, have disguised a love poem of his own by placing it in the mouth of a fictitious character? To whom, female or male, do these shining but fickle eyes and compliant body belong?

> A naked form that reaches out
> Desiring what could never be, it seemed.
> Eyes alight with joy unbounded,
> 'How are a diamond's carats to be counted?'

> Arms so limp in my battering embraces
> Flesh bent to my body any way I wish
> And huge eyes so frank, especially when they lie,
> 'Water down your tears for me to lick away.'

The 'form' cannot be that of Ellen, who had almost hurled herself at Marcueil. The erotic part of the poem continues for two more verses with the pronoun *elle* of the third verse still referring back to the *forme* of the first line. Nor is the French possessive pronoun *sa* any guide to whether the subject of the poem is male or female, as its gender is only governed by the following noun. The extra line of the fifth verse breaks the erotic atmosphere:

> Just as Adam, inspired by a double draught of breath
> Awakes to find Eve by his side,
> When sleep deserts me, I discover Helen,
> The old but eternal name by which beauty goes,
> Squeaked out on a trumpet through the mists of time.[21]

In the squeaky note of the trumpet proclaiming Helen's (not Ellen's) beauty, Jarry betrays his own ambivalent attitude towards female beauty. He was sceptical of archaic models such as Helen of Troy or Venus. 'Do we really know if our admiration for the ancient statues of Venus is down to anything except tradition?' he would query in a future article.[22]

Pierre Bonnard, Ink drawing for a 1902 advertisement in *La Revue blanche* announcing Jarry's novel *Le Surmâle*.

Taken outside the context of *Le Surmâle* (for the 'lying eyes' cannot be the adoring Ellen's), this poem ranks alongside *Madrigal* as Jarry's most intimate and certainly his most erotic poem. The gender of the beloved is deliberately left open, but a fickle Bougrelas from Montmartre cannot be discounted. If the poem relates to a real erotic encounter, it would enliven the bleak landscape of Jarry's emotional life, about which his published correspondence reveals so little.

The violent *dénouement* of *Le Surmâle* further proves how disconnected Marcueil's verses are from the plot. Perceiving that Marcueil is not in love with his daughter, Elson instructs the engineer, Arthur Gough, to construct an electro-magnetic Love-inspiring Machine, to which the naked man, still semi-conscious, is attached. Ellen has by now recovered. Gough is not certain that such a hasty construction will work, but Elson insists on trying it out immediately. Indeed the Supermale's innate power throws the current into reverse. This causes the platinum bands round his head and the insulating glass plate to overheat and melt, causing glass 'tears' to run down his face. (Jarry had already described the two Americans trying to blot out the obvious image of Christ in his crown of thorns, nailed to the cross, before they had turned on the current.) Marcueil's agony is so unbearable that he breaks free of his bonds. The final vignette of the Supermale is of his burned corpse intertwined with the metal bars of the gate through which he had tried to escape.

It was a mischievous writerly tic of Jarry's to give his athletic male protagonists some of his own characteristics. They were his fantasy alter egos. Like him, Mnester and Marcueil have tiny feet. Both are emotionally cold and destroyed through the agency of a predatory woman. Although Jarry had close female friends in Rachilde, Fanny Zaessinger and his later puppet partner, Berthe Danville, he remained convinced of the potential destructive power of a woman in love.

From the beginning of 1900 to the end of 1902 Jarry's regular income from *La Revue blanche* allowed him an independent existence outside Paris, where he could fish, cycle and go boating on the river. These two years were probably the most stable and contented period of his adult life. Puppet performances of *Ubu* would twice take him back to the city, however. On 27 November 1901 he joined forces with the Champs-Élysées puppeteer, Anatole, to produce *Ubu sur la Butte*, a much reduced two-act version of *Ubu Roi* adapted for glove puppets at the Guignol des 4-z' Arts. According to Anatole, the puppets were manipulated by Ernest Labelle.[23] Jarry's own expertise was in operating stringed marionettes. The play ran for an astounding 64 performances.

The head of the surviving Ubu glove puppet, now preserved at the Musée des Arts et Traditions Populaires may have been sculpted by Paul-François Berthoud, usually responsible for heads of the Théâtre des Gueules de Bois puppets,[24] yet Edmond Couturier's 1903 sketch of the Ubu puppet manipulated by Jarry at the Pantins bears much more similarity to the sharp-nosed glove puppet than to the squashy features of the Véritable Marionnette, dated to 1897. The head of the glove puppet, although constantly repainted, still has

Père Ubu glove puppet, wood and cloth, made for the 1901 production of *Ubu sur la Butte* at the Guignol des 4-z' Arts, Paris, and now in the Musée des Arts et Traditions Populaires, Paris.

an indentation in the middle of the crown, as if a wire had entered that spot. Couturier's drawing shows a wire attached to the head of Jarry's puppets, but unfortunately the late date of his drawing does not help to ascertain which of the two Ubu puppets he drew.

Even before the success of *Ubu sur la Butte*, and although he was almost allergic to leaving Paris and its environs, Jarry had already accepted an invitation to give a lecture and a performance of the Pantins puppets at the Libre Esthétique Salon in Brussels. This took place on 22 March 1902. Jarry took advantage of the occasion to play excerpts not only of *Ubu Roi*, but of his unperformed *Les Silènes* and Franc-Nohain's censored *Vive la France!* This particular invitation to avant-garde French authors had previously been extended to Villiers de l'Isle Adam and to Mallarmé and was a great honour. It came from the art critic Octave Maus, director of the Libre d'Esthéthique, through the intervention of Demolder, who escorted Jarry throughout his stay and even helped him in the performance. He was also assisted by the Brussels puppeteer Sander Pierron, who, nearly thirty years after the event, wrote an amusing account of Jarry's stay.[25]

Pierron's claim that Jarry remained in Brussels for a mere 24 hours has been disputed.[26] A one-line greeting on a postcard post-marked 16 March to Claudius-Jacquet, seemingly ever present in his thoughts, implies that Jarry probably arrived on 15 March. He would have left on 22 March, the day after the performance. He had time to visit the Musée Royal des Beaux Arts and see Breughel's *Massacre of the Innocents*, which he would use to support his argument against historical reconstitution in his lecture, *Le Temps dans l'art*, only two weeks later. He also went to see a puppet performance at the Toone theatre, of which he wrote an enthusiastic account.[27]

Pierron wrote a detailed description of Jarry. He credits him with looking much younger than his thirty years. As he walked along with Pierron and Demolder, the writer's girlish appearance, his long hair, 'high crystalline voice' and tapping heels caused heads to turn. His city attire consisted of a soft felt hat, a thread-bare black suit, topped with an ample but ragged bow tie. Over this he wore a short hooded cape. Unsurprisingly, his detachable collar and cuffs did not come up to Pierron's standards of whiteness. In the place of cufflinks Jarry had adopted a knot of blue wool to secure one cuff and a knot of red in the other – a rather modern solution. He was shod in a pair of women's long button boots with a narrow Louis xv heel – no doubt Rachilde's – in which he was taking very tiny steps, prompting Demolder to tell him he was mincing like a tart.

At his lecture Jarry's opening words were: 'Ladies and gentlemen, I realize I've been brought here to say the word to you, but the word should not merely be said, it should be bellowed . . . *merdre!*'[28] Georges Eekhoud later wrote of 'our little *fast women*' who don't like to be discomfited by anything and who fiercely sat out the lashes of Jarry's humour.[29] Pierron claims that some of the audience made for the door, but that Jarry's explanation that the word *merdre* had merely been the signal for the attack against King Wenceslas in his play, reassured them. According to Pierron, the rest of the lecture was an unmitigated success and his friends had difficulty prising him away from the perfumed ladies who encircled him afterwards.

The writer Georges Eekhoud was Jarry's third companion on this trip. His novel *Escal-Vigor*, with its unequivocally homosexual heroes, had prompted his arrest in September 1900. Jarry had been one of the eighty French writers who signed the letter of protest published in *La Revue blanche* declaring his arrest to be an attack on the liberty of expression in the arts.[30] Jarry had known Eekhoud for some time. He was not only a Mercure de France author, but had been translating Marlowe's *Edward II* for Lugné-Poe during Jarry's tenure at the Théâtre de l'Œuvre.[31]

After the lecture, at Jarry's request, his three Belgian companions took him to try the regional beers. As the tally mounted, Eekhoud had to call a halt and they moved on to the annual dinner of a photography club, where Jarry was expected. After demolishing pea soup and fish, Jarry had pushed his plate away believing the dinner had finished. When thick slices of roast beef arrived, he claimed he never ate meat. He none the less pressed on politely with beef, chicken and tart, helped down with the regional beer, lambic. By two o'clock in the morning Demolder and Jarry were incapable of standing upright. Fortunately a horse-drawn cab appeared. Pierron finally had to carry Jarry into his hotel. It would be surprising if some photographs of this momentous evening and of the photography circle's famous guest do not eventually emerge from a forgotten album.

The Brussels trip was Jarry's third and last abroad and also the last time that he was so comprehensively fêted. The loss of his regular column in *La Revue blanche* at the end of 1902 seemed to represent a watershed in his career. His contributions to other journals still gave him an income and he also continued to cultivate an image of sporting achievement. None the less his alcohol consumption increased, he ate little, and the last four years of his life show a pattern of declining health.

10

Poverty, Illness and Death

The last chapter of Jarry's life is not a happy one, but it is a mistake to project the picture of a poverty-stricken and sick alcoholic on to his earlier years. By the beginning of 1903 his alcoholism had certainly become acute. The fact that he survived for nearly five more years is a credit to his toughness, for he was afflicted with frequent bouts of influenza, possibly a sign of the incipient tuberculosis that killed him. The year 1903 began with one of these bouts. The cold, damp conditions of his riverside hovel can only have aggravated his vulnerability, but by now he was attached to his Coudray routine and began to nurture a dream of owning his own piece of land there. It is typical of Jarry that lack of funds did not deter him from achieving this ambition.

Letters from Coudray during the winter months prove that he far preferred his chilly, independent existence in the country to his urban one. He enjoyed drinking with the local fishermen and made a list of their colourful nicknames, among them Mal-au-Ventre, Cul-de-Rat, Pomme Cuite and Grandes-Moustaches.[1] Here there was no need to keep up appearances, whereas his increasing shabbiness provoked comment in the Paris cafés and bars, frequented by writers who, knowing his earlier reputation, expected him to be a more flamboyant figure. Although Jarry sporadically attended Paul Fort's gatherings at the Closerie des Lilas in the years 1904–6, he sometimes remained determinedly silent.[2]

Pablo Picasso,
Alfred Jarry,
reproduced in
Les Soirées de Paris,
February 1914.

Dessin de Picasso.

ALFRED JARRY

If Jarry was easily bored, he none the less responded to original talent. He had inspired the allegiance of four younger writers, who would make their mark on the twentieth century: Guillaume Apollinaire, F. T. Marinetti, Max Jacob and André Salmon. For them Jarry's tramp-like attire and squalid apartment represented less of a reduction in circumstances than a defiant artistic statement. They recorded each detail with reverence. Of the four writers, Apollinaire seems to have established the closest rapport with Jarry.

Before the collapse of *La Revue blanche*, Fénéon had already given Jarry an introduction to *La Plume* and it was for them that he wrote some of his most original articles in 1903. He also made a point of attending *La Plume*'s Saturday *soirées*, literary evenings preceded by a dinner and presided over by each of the journal's writers in turn. It was at the first of these on 18 April 1903 that Jarry and Apollinaire met formally. Jarry's own turn to preside came on 16 May, when he recited his poem 'Bardes et cordes', with all the rhymes in '–ardes' and '–ordes', an almost Mallarméan exercise, which struck Apollinaire forcefully. The 23-year-old poet took to Jarry and may not have wanted to share him with Picasso. He is suspected of being equally possessive about the painter, and of fearing to lose some of his power over him by introducing him to someone more sensitive to new trends in art than he was.[3] Extraordinarily, the lack of a formal introduction may be what kept Jarry and Picasso apart.

At their first meeting Jarry had impressed Apollinaire straight away by reciting verses from two of his poems by heart. Jarry's colourful tales of his drunken escapades found an avid listener. After the dinner and a game of billiards, Apollinaire claims to have returned home with Jarry at three o'clock in the morning.[4] If fishing provided the extra-literary bond between Jarry and Vallette, billiards provided a similar one between Jarry and Apollinaire and a subject of the correspondence between them.

The role of Apollinaire in the removal of Jarry's gun after the shooting incident at Maurice Raynal's house remains uncertain. If we believe his account, Jarry had to collect it from the atelier of a mutual friend in Montmartre six months later. The chances are that this mutual friend was Picasso, but there is no evidence for this. After Jarry's death, Vallette drew up a tally of his possessions in an effort to reduce the debts that would pass to his sister. He mentions a revolver that was not only in pawn but, like his bicycle, not even fully paid for.[5] Jarry's distress at parting from his gun is reflected in a passage of his semi-autobiographical novel *La Dragonne*, in which Erbrand de Sacqueville, the last of his fictitious selves, muses bitterly on the loss of his revolver, sold to fund his drink habit, speaking of it as a kind of talisman which had not only given him power, but protection from what he called 'the outer darkness':

In order to drink more and all the time, he pawned his family jewels . . . And it came to the point when he even had to sell the Thing which, through a tiny, sovereign movement of his index finger, made him prince of the outer darkness and master of everyone's life, everywhere and always: his revolver.[6]

Picasso almost certainly acquired Jarry's revolver after his death, possibly for the second time. There is at least one account of him brandishing it when he took Fernande Olivier to Catalonia.[7] Max Jacob's story that Jarry gave it to him is, however, likely to be apocryphal.

Apollinaire was one of the few to keep Jarry's memory alive, designating him 'the last of the great burlesque poets' and calling for his woodcuts, which he described as 'almost cabbalistic in character', to be republished.[8] After Jarry's death he also converted his first diary impressions of the writer he had looked up to into a vivid portrait:

> Alfred Jarry . . . appeared to me as the personification of a river, a young smooth-chinned river, clad in the soaking wet clothes of a drowned man. His wispy, drooping moustache, the frock-coat whose tails swung to and fro, his baggy shirt and cycling shoes, all had something soft and spongy about them; the demi-god was still damp. He looked as if he had emerged dripping wet from his river bed only a few hours earlier.[9]

A rather less romanticized portrait of the writer was left by Marinetti, founder of the later Futurist movement. Only three years younger than Jarry, he esteemed him as a fellow tradition-breaker. Jarry's perception of the interrelatedness of humans and machines and his imaginative inventions, such as the Love-inspiring Machine of *Le Surmâle*, had a powerful influence on Marinetti. He refers to

Jarry as 'an unquestionable genius of the underworld' and enjoyed introducing his threadbare friend into the most elegant salons, causing tremors of horror. Noting the writer's mannerism of using string to hold his clothes together, he pronounced Jarry's dress to be 'a flagrant banner of voluntary poverty' proclaiming 'a gratuitous way of life in a very prosperous Paris'.[10]

In 1905 Marinetti commissioned Jarry to write two articles for his magazine *Poesia*: the first, 'Le Fouzi-Yama', proposed the famous Japanese volcano as an ancient repository of gunpowder and Japan's secret weapon. (Could Roald Dahl have had knowledge of this article when he wrote the screenplay for a Bond film, *You Only Live Twice*?) The second, 'Lyrisme militaire', speculated on the potential of kites for military spying. Apollinaire would meanwhile commission Jarry's playlet *L'Objet aimé* for his journal *Le Festin d'Ésope*. Both he and Marinetti drew heavily from *Ubu Roi* for their own plays: in Marinetti's case, *Le Roi Bombance*, performed in 1909, and in Apollinaire's, *Les Mamelles de Tirésias* of 1917. Marinetti sent the text of his play to Jarry in July 1906, prompting a long, appreciative letter. 'Your treatment of surprise', wrote Jarry, 'is not aimed so much at laughter as the horrifyingly beautiful.'[11] The writer who had once given his definition of a monster as 'any original, inexhaustible beauty'[12] recognized a kindred spirit.

Within the context of *La Plume*'s literary banquets, where younger writers looked up to him, Jarry had every right to feel that he had finally reached a position of eminence. Unfortunately *La Plume* only lasted till January 1904. He then had to fall back on the *Canard sauvage* and *L'Œil*, both edited by Franc-Nohain, his friend and puppet partner from the Pantins. *L'Œil* folded in August and the *Canard sauvage* in October. For a few weeks in the summer he was invited to contribute to *Le Figaro* under the heading *Fantaisies parisiennes*. In a letter to Apollinaire he even describes himself as 'glittering with Figaro gold'.[13] The story goes that he was rebuked for bringing in his third article late and tore it up, slamming the door as he left. It still exists in manuscript, but Jarry often wrote several copies. The rents from the two Laval properties that he shared with his sister would now provide his only regular income. The various little *opéras-bouffes* suggested by Claude Terrasse were potentially lucrative, if only they could be brought to production. Indeed Jarry's final windfall came from the ever optimistic and generous Terrasse.

Jarry had a great facility for rhyme and what he called *mirliton-esque* verse. The *mirliton* or kazoo is the small pipe that puppeteers use to give their voice its characteristic squeaky timbre. Jarry took pleasure in writing the frivolous pieces, perhaps turning to them as a relief from the more serious work that he was doing at the same time. Under the rubric of *Théâtre Mirlitonesque*, three of his *opéras-bouffes*, were finally published by Sansot in 1906 in a series of six volumes, along with *Ubu sur la Butte*, *Ubu intime* and a collection of his previous articles.

Terrasse had quickly recognized Jarry's potential for libretti and hoped to bind the writer's talent to his own more firmly than turned out to be the case. Eugène Demolder had to be brought into the team to shore up Jarry's resolve and to help with the actual writing, which took up more and more of his time. Most of the scores that Terrasse wrote for Jarry's *opéras-bouffes* are missing as are many variants of the texts. Even the versions that have come to light did not surface until the middle of the twentieth century. Of them all, only two were actually performed: *Léda* in May 1900 and *Le Manoir enchanté* in January 1905.

The interminable *Pantagruel* project had been begun in 1898 and had already undergone numerous drafts. Terrasse and Jarry had originally conceived it as a five-act puppet play for the Pantins, following the plot of Rabelais' Five Books. It was to cause increasing friction between the two men. Terrasse's diary entries for 1900 mention his anxieties about the work sixteen times. At the end of 1900 he first uses the term 'libretto' in a letter to Jarry, indicating their decision to change genres and make

Pantagruel into a wholly sung work. At the same time he gave up the premises in rue Ballu previously used for the Pantins.[14] Between 1900 and 1904 Jarry seems to have undertaken a complete restructuring of the work, collapsing Rabelais' Five Books into a synthesis of Books I and V.[15] He deeply resented the time spent on this.

In a gesture that was both compassionate and in his own creative interest, Terrasse had 'captured' Jarry straight after the demise of *La Plume* at the beginning of 1904 and taken him to his house in Le Grand-Lemps in the Dauphiné, a rural region between Lyon and Grenoble. A mere two weeks after arriving Jarry writes to Rachilde declaring that he will be back within a fortnight. He complains that he dislikes the mountains and does not feel at home. It was after this stay, actually four months later, that a host of empty bottles of mouthwash, an alcohol substitute, were discovered in Jarry's bathroom. This was in addition to the bottles that were cleared from under his bed each day.[16] It was not even as if he was confined to the house, for he went on long cycling trips and indulged his passion for billiards in the local cafés, where he was far from tee-total. Terrasse's generosity and patience with Jarry was to be taxed to the limit, for at the end of the four months Jarry decided that, as far as he was concerned, *Pantagruel* was finished and that he was not going to put any more work into it. It was, after all, eight years since he had embarked on it.

On 9 November 1904 Demolder had written to André Fontainas that he and Jarry had been summoned to the Dauphiné by Terrasse to finish writing *Le Manoir enchanté*. A period of ten days was envisaged, but Demolder wrote again on 11 December to say that the actor, Deplé, had demanded changes. 'We've worked like blacks till midnight, two or three a.m. every day! It's done! I can rest – at least until tomorrow. We've had to put in comic episodes that have changed the whole thing. It's complete comedy now . . .'.[17] An undated letter from Fernand Depas, the potential director, asks urgently for '*visible* modifications' to the operetta, promising to double Jarry's share of the takings for the imminent evening's performance, in view of the fact that the task would be on top of what had already been agreed with him.[18] The financial potential of the work was of great importance to Jarry. A successful operetta brought in as much in one night as Terrasse earned in a month from his music lessons at 6 rue Ballu.[19]

It is likely that Jarry's share of the takings from *Le Manoir enchanté*, in addition to a sum that he received for the publication of a Czech translation of *Messaline*, enabled him to achieve his great ambition of acquiring his own plot of land by the Coudray weir, a very short distance from the Vallette's villa. The act of sale was signed on 23 December 1904 before the Corbeil notary and Jarry spent a cold Christmas at Corbeil, revelling in his purchase. A month later, on 24 January, he paid the sum of 325 francs to the vendors, Monsieur and Madame Rioux.[20] Upon this plot the proud structure of Jarry's 'Tripode' would gradually be erected on its *four* legs. At last he was a proprietor in his own right, but the tiny wooden house, whose dimensions of 3.69 x 3.69 metres Jarry may have hoped had a beneficial magical significance, was not to be completed for some eighteen months.

Terrasse meanwhile despaired of getting Jarry's further co-operation on *Pantagruel.* In April 1905 he finally agreed to pay the writer an advance of 3,000 francs for his author's rights, a payment that was notarized with the Société des Auteurs Dramatiques. Was this the 3,000 francs that Jarry told the caretaker of 7 rue Cassette that he had received from his sister and from which he took 1,800 francs to have an up to the minute flushing lavatory installed?[21]

During 1905 Jarry was travelling backwards and forwards from Paris, either to his sister in Laval, or to his maternal uncles in Lamballe, near Saint-Brieuc. He was collecting material for his novel *La Dragonne*, the project to which he devoted the end of his life. It was far nearer to his heart than the endless grind on *Pantagruel*, which he accused of undermining his health. While still at the peak of his creative ability, he had published a chapter of *La Dragonne* in *La Revue blanche* in 1903. This chapter, titled 'La Bataille de Morsang', is the only one whose authenticity is certain. Inspired by the village of Morsang-sur-Seine near Coudray, it is also the only one written before Jarry's terrible decline in health.

In this chapter, the character Erbrand de Sacqueville has been rejected by Jeanne de Sabrenas, who has been brought up as a soldier, but is also the regimental whore. In revenge Erbrand plots to massacre the regiment on the march through cunning use of geometry. He chooses a circular site for his 'battle', semi-enclosed by a horse-shoe bend in the river. His 'camouflage' is a green waterproof fisherman's cape, such as Jarry himself wore. It is pitch dark and the infantry follow the bank of the river until they are disposed in a wide circle. Erbrand, barking an order, imitates the general. A gun is fired by mistake, causing a multiple echo and fears of an ambush. Conflicting orders to fire are given. Erbrand places himself at the precise centre of the circular field, where bullets aimed by the soldiers at the circumference towards the invisible 'enemy' supposedly three hundred metres away, either pass over his head or to each side of him. The regiment eventually destroys itself, while Erbrand is safe at the nucleus of the cyclone of bullets.

In a gruesome and sexually sadistic scene Erbrand then executes Jeanne, piercing her between the breasts with his sword. He throws her into the river, where her bloated body is found by fishermen. In a macabre transposition of mouth and vulva, Jarry makes Jeanne's vulva break the surface first and take a gulp of air 'like a goldfish gulping a crumb of cake', making a little kissing noise as if it were saying 'Hello' to the fishermen. This is the most savagely misogynistic passage of Jarry's entire œuvre.[22] In fact the whole chapter is a coldly logical working out of violent fantasies. By comparison, the section of the novel devoted to Erbrand's Breton past appears quite sentimental, in what seems to be an affectionate resurrection of the characters and elderly relatives who peopled Jarry's childhood.

Parts of *La Dragonne* were dictated to Charlotte while Jarry was too ill to write; other sections were added by her from memory and cannot be regarded as his own composition; others again are known to have been written by Jarry, but are wrongly credited to Charlotte in the first published edition. Multiple versions of the manuscript exist in fragments that differ from each other. Vallette returned the version sent to him as being *informe* (shapeless). Jarry repeatedly declared that his novel was finished. This was either to cover up his inability to finish it, much as he disguised his ill health, or, as one commentator believes, his perception of 'complete' corresponded to what others might consider 'shapeless', and that the novel might even represent a new genre.[23]

The huge critical task of deciphering the variants of *La Dragonne* left by Jarry and of transcribing his multiple plans, notes and newspaper cuttings has yet to be addressed. Gravely ill in May 1906, he wrote to Rachilde in the hope that 'the writer he admired most in the world' would take the 'three-quarters finished' novel over together with its huge box of notes and complete it either in her own way or as a 'posthumous collaboration'. Rachilde sensibly refused.

Throughout his life and especially during the drab final years of illness and poverty, Jarry's letters to Rachilde painted a colourful and amusing picture, always providing an upbeat chronicle of his achievements. A lively vein runs through their correspondence and her humorous admonishments of his lifestyle lifted his morale. He also looked to her as the most astute judge of his work. His poem 'Madrigal', published in *La Revue blanche* of February 1903, prompted her most encouraging letter of all. The poem is supposedly written to a young prostitute. He calls her 'Messaline', but she is not the predatory Messalina of his novel. She is an exhausted child, whom the poet approaches with an almost religious respect,

Manuscript of the poem 'Le Mousse de la Pirrouït', an extract from *La Dragonne*.

requiring only her undivided attention, not sexual favours. In its evocation of intimacy, the poem is a rare example of lyricism from Jarry's pen:

> My little girl, sleep tight at last.
> You belong to everyone, so that includes me.
> No one was your valid master,
> Let's close the window and go to sleep:
> Life has shut down and we are at home.[24]

All too aware of her friend's shortcomings, Rachilde speculates ruefully on the number of girls and the quantity of pure alcohol that Jarry would need in order to produce an entire volume of similar verse. Tongue in cheek, the novelist, whose reputation had been built on her unusually virile approach to sexual subjects, claims coyly not to know Jarry's world. Jarry's huge consumption of alcohol horrified her. In her memoir she made a tally of his drinking, as she recalled it:

> Jarry began the day by imbibing two litres of white wine; between ten and twelve he would down three absinthes, then at lunch he would moisten his fish or his steak with red or white wine, alternating with more absinthes. In the afternoon there would be cups of coffee together with liqueurs or various types of alcohol, whose names I forget, then at dinner, after other aperitifs of course, he would take at least two more bottles of any vintage, regardless of the label.[25]

If correct, this amount of alcohol would be formidable for any man to process. For one of Jarry's small stature it should have been lethal, yet he lived on, even as his ability to afford food declined. His apparent invulnerability matched the myth of the Supermale that he had created for himself and for Erbrand de Sacqueville:

He drank alone and methodically, without ever managing to get drunk and without any possibility of ever becoming what is fashionably known today as an alcoholic: his doses were so vast that they slipped between his cells like a vanishing river, as it filters through the eternal and indifferent sand: otherwise Erbrand would have long since been dead.[26]

As his health deteriorated, it became impossible for Jarry to sustain writing projects on his own. After turning his back on *Pantagruel* he began a collaborative project with his Paris-based doctor, Jean Saltas, to translate a Greek novel on Pope Joan by Emmanuel Rhoïdes, which would become *La Papesse Jeanne.* He had an ambivalent relationship with Saltas, who both admired and pitied him. His return to Paris was not only because the river-side stable had become too uncomfortable in winter, but because his local creditors had become importunate. Now he spent his days working on his translation in the warm dry conditions of the Bibliothèque Nationale with dictionaries in easy reach. Saltas writes of him stopping off on his way home, whereupon he would slip a heated brick under his wet feet while they worked and give him hot cups of tea and food to go with it; but this was not a routine.[27] Jarry's letters to the doctor at the end of 1905 and the first half of 1906 constantly postpone appointments.

Saltas was in awe of his famous patient. Jarry, on the other hand, privately referred to him as a fool. The publisher Eugène Fasquelle had insisted on his delivering *La Dragonne* before he would take on *La Papesse Jeanne.* In a fit of paranoia, Jarry wrote to Fénéon that although he was at death's door Saltas had been pressurizing him to finish *La Dragonne*, so that he, Saltas, could bask in the glory of publishing *La Papesse Jeanne*.[28] Jarry had suffered the same paranoia about Terrasse and *Pantagruel.* Saltas, by contrast, does not have a bad word to say about his collaborator. He recalls him as punctilious about returning the tiniest sums. Jarry was at his most destitute at this period. Saltas had met him on an errand to sell his precious resource of books. The ceiling-high mountain remembered by Apollinaire was gradually being eroded.

Jarry depended on Saltas for palliatives to soothe his frequent toothache, and for sending him minor medical supplies while in Laval. The doctor was concerned about his alcohol consumption, but Jarry was keen to play down the role of drink in his illness: 'Père Ubu, as people call me, is not dying from having drunk too much, but from not always having eaten. You, meanwhile, made me eat at teatime. Thank you.'[29] Hardly eating, Jarry was struggling with *La Dragonne* at the same time as the Greek translation and the volumes for Sansot. According to his letters, he often worked through the night. A candle was then his only light. In cycling to and from the Bibliothèque Nationale he was frequently drenched. Fatigue, chills and an underlying illness, of which he was ignorant, were wearing him down.

However weak, Jarry never failed to attend Rachilde's *mardis* and the Vallettes could not help but notice his deterioration. In May 1906 they procured him a train ticket to Laval to recover his health. They also mobilized his old colleague, Adolphe van Bever from the Théâtre de l'Œuvre, to wake him up and make sure that he caught the morning train of 11 May. In order to retain the rental income from 13 and 15 rue de Bootz, Charlotte had rented a less expensive third-floor apartment near the cathedral, and this is where Jarry went. The Vallettes were relieved he was out of the unhealthy environment of the capital and in the care of his sister. However the apartment was hot and stuffy, being right under the roof.[30] The sense of fatigue did not leave him and he was still suffering from toothache. Although he admits to summoning a doctor, his letters to the Vallettes maintain a forced gaiety and attempt to conceal the fact that he is not recovering. His letters to Saltas are very different. Repeated requests to him for a thermometer imply that he thinks he has a fever. These begin on 19 May.

A fortnight after his arrival, he writes: 'You are too intelligent not to have realized that I was talking through my hat when I announced my sudden recovery (!!!) and return to perfect health in my last letter.'[31] Jarry tells Saltas he cannot yet stomach water, which causes him to vomit. Instead, he is drinking cider sent by his Lamballe uncles, doubtless contrary to the detoxification regime on which the local doctor has put him. No particular medicine seems to have been prescribed. Jarry asks Saltas for quinium, a quinine-based preparation, popularly advertised as effective against fevers, general debility, nervousness and exhaustion.

Jarry finds relief from his illness by writing letters. He says as much to Saltas, calling it a 'cure by correspondence'.[32] His most colourful and unguarded letter of all is written to Rachilde on 28 May, when he believes he is dying and that these will be his last written words:

Dear Madame Rachilde
Père Ubu is not writing in a state of fever this time. (This is beginning like a last will and testament, but that is taken care of.) I think that you will have understood that he is not dying (sorry, that word slipped out) because of drink and other orgies. That was not his passion, and he has immodestly had himself examined from top to bottom by the *merdics.* He has no flaw, either in the liver, or the heart, or the kidneys, or even in the urinary tract! He is simply run down, (a curious end for one who has written *Le Surmâle*), and his boiler is not going to burst but just go out. He is going to come to a stop quite gradually like a worn-out engine . . . And no treatment designed for humans, however faithfully he may follow it (laughing to himself all the while), will be any use. His high fever perhaps comes from the fact that his heart is trying to save him by sending his pulse rate up to 150. No human being has ever held out that long. For the last two days he has been of the Lord's Anointed and,

like Kipling's trunkless elephant, is filled with an insatiable curiosity. He is going to retreat a little further *back* into the night of time. In the same way as he would carry his revolver in his hip pocket, he has had a gold chain put round his neck, for the sole reason that this metal does not oxidize and will last as long as his bones, just in case he meets any devils. This gives him as much fun as going fishing . . . Note that if he doesn't die after all, it will be grotesque to have written all this . . . But we reiterate that this is not written under the influence of fever. He has left such beautiful things on the earth, but is disappearing in an apotheosis like this!

[. . .]

Père Ubu has had a shave and has laid out a mauve shirt (no connection with you intended!) he will disappear in the *Mercure colours*. . . and he will set off still consumed with an insatiable curiosity. He has a feeling that it will happen this evening at five . . . If he's wrong he'll look ridiculous and that's that. Ghosts are ridiculous after all.

So saying, Père Ubu, who has earned his rest, is going to try to sleep. He believes that the brain, in the process of decomposition, carries on working after death and that its dreams are what we think of as Paradise. Père Ubu, and this is conditional – he would so much like to return to his Tripod – is perhaps going to sleep *forever.*

ALFRED JARRY

[. . .]

P.S. I am opening my letter to say that the doctor has just arrived and thinks he can save me.[33]

Although Jarry is careful to keep the tone light-hearted, there is a great deal of self-pity in this letter. At one point he even asks Rachilde to pray for him. All the signs are that he had made up his mind to die. He had dictated his last will and testament to a notary, leaving his goods and authorial rights to Charlotte and his unpaid for Corbeil property to Rachilde. He had also dictated his obituary notice. He states his wish to be buried alongside his mother in the family tomb in Rennes – a wish that, for lack of money would never be fulfilled. He draws up a signed declaration announcing that, being on the point of death, he is unable to conclude his manuscript of *La Dragonne* and that he has dictated the plan to his sister. All these careful preparations are brought to an abrupt halt by the arrival of the doctor. From the tone of Jarry's post scriptum to Rachilde, Dr Bucquet seems to have flatly contradicted his patient's opinion that he only had a few hours to live.

Jarry believed that in the course of his delirium he had descended to Hell and, during an encounter with Lucifer, with the help of the Virgin Mary and Saint Anne, managed to release the fallen archangel from his six-thousand-year imprisonment. In his delirium the Archangel Michael also came to his bedside. It is as if the religious engravings, over which he had pored for *L'Ymagier*, suddenly came to life. A long letter addressed to Rachilde and dictated to Charlotte, but with insertions in his own hand, recounts his vision in a mixture of French, Latin and Greek. Jarry's intention was to make his delirious episode into the final chapter of *La Dragonne*, as an experience of Erbrand's. In a letter to Fénéon he called it 'my little touristic escapade beyond the gates of death'.[34] When he returned to himself, Jarry thought better of posting the account of his visions to Rachilde. The letter was never sent.[35]

Jarry's subsequent letters to the Vallettes and to Saltas are full of apologies for over-dramatizing his state. He disavows the 'cerebral fever' as an effect of an over-active imagination, claiming that Saltas's thermometer had never registered above 37.4 degrees.[36] He admits that it is annoying not to have died, having just put his affairs in order. Dr Bucquet had clearly persuaded him to think positively about recovery and agreed to Jarry going to his riverside 'cottage' for the second half of his convalescence. Jarry now writes of walks

Jarry at Maître Blaviel's fencing school, 1906.

in the fresh air, picnics and cycling.[37] What the doctor does not know are the dreadful conditions in which his patient lives when on his own.

For Jarry there were no half measures. Having decided that he was not going to die, he set about emphasizing his return to good health. Living on as a pitiable, sickly ex-writer was not an option. Vallette is asked to send his bicycle by train from Paris. In July he sends photographs of himself sparring with the local fencing master. This Jarry is far from the lean, athletic figure of the 1898 Phalanstère photographs. Balding and puffy-faced, he looks at least ten years older than his actual age.

Jarry returned to Paris on 26 July after an absence of two and a half months. Vallette had hoped that he would not come back at all. However, his return was timed to coincide with a banquet in honour of the writer Jean Moréas at which all Jarry's literary contacts were present. It was an important event that enabled him to reassert his presence in the literary community of Paris. He had, however, been chafing to return to Coudray. He had after all not yet lived in his newly built 'Tripode'. August 1906 was the first time that he was able to inhabit the little summer house, of which he had been dreaming. Although Demolder's wife reported from her nearby villa that Jarry's hands and feet were less swollen, the clear-sighted Vallette observed that his friend was not cured, and feared for his fate in the winter to come.[38]

With the cooler weather of October, Jarry returned of his own accord to Laval, but only for one month. The next twelve months see him drawn backwards and forwards between the capital, where he is a person of literary standing but hardly eats, and his provincial home, where his sister provides domestic support. He is back in Paris for Christmas thanking Rachilde for sending him a chicken, but the end of January 1907 finds him once more writing from Laval. A bulk order to a Laval wine merchant for 218 litres of wine in February does not augur well for the year to come.[39] The detox

Jarry's 'Tripode' summer house at Coudray.

is at an end. Jarry's letters imply that he will be able to finish his novel more easily in provincial isolation where the clean air helps his health. It was certainly a cold winter, and many of his friends had succumbed to the influenza epidemic sweeping through Paris. After two months of being holed up with his large stock of wine, Jarry decided to return to Paris, where he was threatened with eviction from the rue Cassette. Already besieged by creditors in Laval and forewarned of more trouble in Corbeil from his builder, he requests a letter from Dr Bucquet stating that he must not be disturbed 'on doctor's orders'.

Jarry arrived in Paris on 4 or 5 April. To raise money he had brought with him his manuscripts of *Les Jours et les Nuits*, *L'amour absolu* and *Faustroll.* He was in desperate straits to consider parting with these precious documents. He sold them to Victor Lemasle, a manuscript dealer on the Quai Malaquais. From there they were bought by his old friend and editor, Louis Lormel. Jarry also submitted to Lemasle for publication a small volume of biographical souvenirs on the poet, Albert Samain. It would be the last book published in his lifetime.

Within the week Jarry was too ill to leave his bed. On 16 April he writes for help to a young friend, Victor Gastilleur, who, with Van Bever had helped him catch his train the year before. Gastilleur rushes to the rue Cassette, for Jarry wrote that he had been unable to get provisions for five days. Charlotte had also sent a money order that urgently needed collecting. It is likely that Gastilleur saw to it that Jarry was provided for over the following fortnight. At the very least he was able to obtain him the reduced fare back to Laval, which, Jarry wrote, would save his life.[40] Jarry had not even managed to survive on his own for a month in Paris.

Matters continued to get worse. Despite the fact that Jarry had paid in April the rent that was owed up to 8 January, he could not bring it up to date. His landlord of the half flat in the rue Cassette now served a notice of eviction on him. In the same month Alfred and Charlotte were evicted from their Laval apartment in the rue Charles-Landelle with a full year's rent owing. Their only recourse was to serve notice on their own tenants and reoccupy their family home of 13 and 15 rue de Bootz, cutting off their only source of income. Monsieur Trochon, knowing that Jarry was now within reach, pressed for payment of his Clément deluxe bicycle with renewed vigour. The wine merchant was likewise short of payment for his 218 litres. On the other hand, Jarry noted with pleasure that the tradesmen who had supplied his family at rue de Bootz in the past were treating them with the same respect as when his father had lived there.[41]

For the months of May and June Jarry was more or less bed-bound. He writes to Rachilde that he is indulging in 'orgies of sleep' and channels all his creativity into vast letters to the Vallettes. They are his final link to the literary world and to his very identity as a writer, that he feels is slipping away. His eviction date for the rue Cassette is 8 July and he is concerned for the huge *Pantagruel* manuscript and family photographs that he has left there. He also asks after the Tripode, which, Vallette replies, has vanished into the undergrowth. Jarry receives a letter from his landlord dated 5 July, enclosing his final bill and asking for the return of his keys. The letter must have arrived the following day, for on 6 July he leaves his bed and takes the night train to Paris.

On seeing his young tenant of twelve years' standing reduced to such a frail state, Jarry's elderly landlord is stricken with remorse and allows him a reprieve. The writer is even too weak to deliver a tiny pot of shrimps to Rachilde, which he asks Vallette to collect. Having achieved his aim of maintaining his foothold in Paris and gathered the papers that he wants, he triumphantly takes the train back to Laval a few days later.

Once again, Jarry has to spend the summer in Laval. August is extremely hot. The long absence from his barely occupied Tripode pains him. He would dearly love to be back at Corbeil in the amusing company of the Vallettes, fishing and canoeing with his friend as before. He writes that the willows on the banks of the Mayenne are too small to offer any shade and that he is hardly fishing. He even admits to having given up cycling.[42] He has, however, finished *La Dragonne*, he claims, and has drawn up his selection of the articles to be included in the proposed volume of *La Chandelle verte.*

Jarry had set his heart on returning to Paris and Corbeil in September and informs Vallette of his intentions. On 30 August he claims to have posted the four-hundred-page manuscript of *La Dragonne* to Thadée Natanson for delivery to Fasquelle. Although he urgently needed the promised advance from the publisher, this manuscript neither left Laval, nor has it ever been identified. Hoping to deter Jarry from coming, Vallette writes that Fasquelle is away and lists all the creditors who have been asking after him. He adds all the discouragements that he can think of: fish are scarce; Jarry has no permit; his own boat is damaged.[43] Jarry is not fooled and his letters of September all announce his imminent departure.

The exact date of Jarry's journey to Paris is not certain. His final letter from Laval, dated 5 October, marks his intention to leave two days later. The temperature has dropped and he is feeling the cold. He recollects his childhood illnesses in the same house. There is then an unusual gap in his correspondence. The evidence of his autopsy pointed to a sudden decline in his health a few weeks before his death. The doctor performing it presumed that a chill had been the trigger, but presumed wrongly that a cycling excursion was the cause.[44] Jarry had not been going out. His next and last known letter, dated 26 October, finds him too weak to leave his room at 7 rue Cassette. It is a desperate plea to Thadée Natanson for a half or whole louis.[45]

Saltas was aware of Jarry's condition. He was probably dropping by and was in touch with Vallette. On 29 October Vallette writes to

André Fontainas with a chilling forecast: 'Père Ubu can no longer stand up and I am going to see him today at ten with Dr Saltas to make up his mind (he has in fact already accepted) to go into La Charité hospital – from where it is extremely probable that he will not come out alive.'[46] It was true that Jarry could no longer stand. He had lost the use of his legs and could not drag himself to the door. His friends had to get a locksmith to obtain access. They immediately called a carriage to get him to the hospital.

The story is taken up by a young doctor doing his rounds the following day. Jarry is one of three new admissions, but the matron cannot put her finger on his ailment. She can tell he has not eaten for at least two days. Jarry is not complaining of anything in particular and does not know why he is there. His expression is blank and he appears to have lost his memory. On pulling back the covers the doctor discovers that he has lost control not only of his legs, but his bodily functions. Despite being cleaned up very recently, he has soiled himself again. The smell is terrible.[47] On her later visit Rachilde is unable to tolerate it. Saltas meets her on her way out. 'He smells of death', she tells him, confessing that she cannot face going back to see him again.[48]

Jarry died on 1 November, All Saints' Day, at 4.15 in the afternoon, only two days after being admitted to hospital. On the first day Terrasse, Franc-Nohain and a recent female admirer, Marie Huot, came to see him. On 31 November his close friends from the Mercure de France came as a band: the Vallettes, Octave Mirbeau, Alexandre Natanson, Van Bever and Georges Polti. Apollinaire and Rachilde relate that Polti was too stricken by Jarry's condition to speak. 'Well, Polti', cried Jarry suddenly, making him jump, 'how are you?'[49] Jarry's sudden rally may be a nice invention. Others relate that Jarry was too far gone to follow the conversation around him.

Saltas was with Jarry when he died. Some speculate as to whether Jarry's whispered last request to him, which he understood as a *cure-dents* (toothpick) was not in fact a *cureton* (priest). The toothpick has become a part of the Jarry legend. Having rushed out to buy a packet, Saltas claimed that, as his friend took one, an expression of joy crossed his face. He turned away for a moment to talk to the nurse. When he turned back, Jarry was dead.

Epilogue

Dr Stéphen-Chauvet, performing the autopsy on Jarry, found, as he expected, the signs of chronic alcoholism in the writer's internal organs. He also found a chronic tubercular patch at the apex of Jarry's right lung. But the real cause of death lay in Jarry's brain and explains his blank expression, his loss of memory and difficulty in answering questions, noted by the doctor on his first examination. The exposed brain revealed the typical lesions of tubercular meningitis. The doctor deduced that the tubercular bacilli must have suddenly spread from his lung as a result of a chill.[1]

Having hardly ventured out the whole summer, Jarry must have made an extreme effort in undertaking the journey to Paris. Is it possible that he wanted to die there, where the literary elite would make his funeral into an event? The fact that his grave would only be a temporary one in the paupers' cemetery of Le Bagneux and that his bones would be thrown into the Fossé Commun would have pained him. He had wanted to be laid to rest in the family tomb of the Quernests in Rennes, whose name he gave in its grand Celtic form as Kernec'h Coutouly de Dorset. Vallette had raised a subscription to cover the Paris funeral, but Charlotte did not have the funds even to extend his grave term at Le Bagneux when it lapsed after five years.

Jarry's funeral took place on Sunday, 3 November. He was lying in an open coffin in an outer part of the hospital, where participants were to meet at 3 pm. The invitation had been issued in the name of Charlotte Jarry, and Jarry's uncles, aunts and cousins on his mother's side. A twenty-minute service was held at the church of Saint-Sulpice. Apollinaire recalled about fifty people in the funeral cortège. Careful to evoke the lively spirit of his friend, he allowed no gloom to darken his record of the event. 'Nobody wept behind Père Ubu's hearse', he wrote. Looking away from the cortège to the pleasure gardens around the Bagneux cemetery, he evoked a merry picture, one that Rachilde repeated in her own memoir. As it was a Sunday and the day after All Souls' Day, the gardens were full of families who had come to attend to their relatives' graves. 'People were singing, drinking and eating charcuterie', wrote Apollinaire, 'a bright and gaudy picture, which could have come straight from the imagination of the person we were taking to rest.'[2]

With the production of *Ubu Roi* in December 1896 something changed in the cultural atmosphere. A seed had been sown. The play stood at the very edge of the performable and posed many risks. Its language was coarse; its crude and violent comedy broke all the rules of what was supposed to entertain; its originality was out of all proportion to what could be tolerated. Looking back at it, the artists and writers of the future avant-garde felt challenged. Jarry's imagination pushed at extremes and he applied it to his lifestyle. He would want to be remembered as the mystery cyclist that amazed passengers could sometimes glimpse racing against their speeding train.

References

Prologue

1 André Gide, *Romans, récits et soties: œuvres lyriques* (Paris, 1958), pp. 1170–71.
2 Maurice Raynal, 'Coups de feu chez moi', *Le Minotaure*, I (1933), pp. 2–3.
3 Guillaume Apollinaire, *Les Contemporains pittoresques: Feu Alfred Jarry* (1909), in *Œuvres en prose complètes* (Paris, 1977–93), vol. II, p. 1041.
4 Alfred Jarry, *Œuvres complètes*, ed. Michel Arrivé, Henri Bordillon, Patrick Besnier and Bernard Le Doze (Paris, 1972–1988), vol. III, p. 590.
5 Max Jacob, draft for *Chroniques des temps héroïques*, cited by Hélène Seckel in *Max Jacob et Picasso* (Quimper, 1994), p. 50.
6 Pierre Daix, *Dictionnaire Picasso* (Paris, 1995), p. 489.
7 Hélène Parmelin, *Picasso sur place* (Paris, 1959), p. 242.

1 Laval, Saint-Brieuc and Rennes

1 *Notes de Charlotte Jarry sur Alfred Jarry*, in Alfred Jarry, *Œuvres complètes*, ed. Michel Arrivé, Henri Bordillon, Patrick Besnier and Bernard Le Doze (Paris, 1972–1988), vol. III, p. 702.
2 Ibid., III, p. 701.
3 Ibid., III, p. 700.
4 Noël Arnaud, *Alfred Jarry, d'Ubu roi au docteur Faustroll* (Paris, 1974), pp. 288–93.
5 Rachilde, *Alfred Jarry, ou le Surmâle des lettres* (Paris, 1928), p. 32.
6 *Œuvres complètes*, p. 702.
7 Ibid., III, p. 702.

8 Henri Bordillon, *Gestes et opinions d'Alfred Jarry, écrivain* (Laval, 1986), p. 21.

9 Rachilde, *Alfred Jarry*, pp. 31–2.

10 Bordillon, *Gestes et opinions d'Alfred Jarry*, p. 35.

11 *Œuvres complètes*, vol. I, p. 933.

12 Henri Bordillon, 'En marge de *l'Amour absolu*', *L'Étoile-Absinthe*, 13–14 (1982), p. 35.

13 *Œuvres complètes*, I, pp. 86–7.

14 Ibid., III, pp. 700 and 701.

15 Ibid., I, p. 778.

16 Ibid., p. 761.

17 Cited in Bordillon, *Gestes et opinions d'Alfred Jarry*, p. 29.

18 Henri Hertz, 'Alfred Jarry, collégien et la naissance d'*Ubu Roi*', reprinted in *L'Étoile-Absinthe*, 51–52 (1992) pp. 5–7.

19 *Œuvres complètes*, III, p. 702.

20 Hertz, 'Alfred Jarry', p. 7.

21 Michel Arrivé, *Les Langages de Jarry. Essai de sémiotique littéraire* (Paris, 1972), pp. 255–6.

22 Maurice Saillet, ed., *Tout Ubu* (Paris, 1962), p. 22.

23 Jean-Paul Goujon, 'De la Pologne et des Polonais,' *L'Étoile-Absinthe*, 31–2 (1986), p. 34.

24 *Œuvres complètes*, III, p. 700.

25 Arnaud, *Alfred Jarry*, p. 112.

26 *Œuvres complètes*, III, p. 702.

2 Literary Success and a Rejected Coat

1 Alfred Jarry, *Œuvres complètes*, ed. Michel Arrivé, Henri Bordillon, Patrick Besnier and Bernard Le Doze (Paris, 1972–1988), vol. III, p. 703.

2 C. Gandilhon Gens-d'Armes, 'Alfred Jarry au Lycée Henri IV', *Les Marges*, XXIII/91 (1922), reprinted in *L'Étoile-Absinthe*, 51–52 (1992), p. 12.

3 Charles-Henry Hirsch cited in Noël Arnaud, *Alfred Jarry, d'Ubu roi au docteur Faustroll* (Paris, 1974), p. 34.

4 Interview with Frédéric Lefèvre, *Les Nouvelles Littéraires* (January 1929), cited in Keith Beaumont, *Alfred Jarry: A Critical and Biographical Study* (Leicester, 1984), p. 32

5 Louise Rypko Schub, *Léon-Paul Fargue* (Geneva, 1973), p. 25.

6 Louis Lormel, 'Entre-soi', *La Plume* (October 1897), pp. 605–6.

7 *Œuvres complètes*, I, p. 233.

8 Patrick Besnier, *Alfred Jarry* (Paris, 2005), p. 103.

9 Rypko-Schub, *Léon-Paul Fargue*, pp. 31–2.

10 Alexandre Auriant's notebook cited in Jean-Paul Goujon, *Léon-Paul Fargue* (Paris, 1997), p. 74.

11 Goujon, *Léon-Paul Fargue*, p. 42.

12 *Œuvres complètes*, III, p. 703.

13 Letter to Edouard Julia, 6 May 1893, cited in Arnaud, *Alfred Jarry*, p. 59.

14 Besnier, *Alfred Jarry*, p. 99.

15 Jarry, *Cahiers Bergson*, Fonds littéraires Jacques Doucet.

16 Rachilde, *Alfred Jarry, ou le Surmâle des lettres* (Paris, 1928), p. 32.

17 Beaumont, *Alfred Jarry*, pp. 176–7.

18 *Cahiers du Collège de 'Pataphysique*, 10 (1953), p. 62.

19 *Œuvres complètes*, I, pp. 181–2.

20 Marguerite Moreno, *Souvenirs de ma vie* (Paris, 1948), p. 78.

21 *Œuvres complètes*, II, p. 626.

22 Remy de Gourmont, 'La Littérature Maldoror', *Mercure de France*, 1 February 1891.

23 *Œuvres complètes*, II, p. 441.

24 Ibid., I, p. 171.

25 Ibid., I, p. 173.

26 Ibid., I, p. 172.

27 *Jarry. Autour d'un testament*, exh. cat. Archives départementales de la Mayenne (Laval, 2007), p. 109.

28 Henri Bordillon, *Gestes et opinions d'Alfred Jarry, écrivain* (Laval, 1986), p. 41.

3 The Art Magazine Editor

1 Alfred Jarry, *Œuvres complètes*, ed. Michel Arrivé, Henri Bordillon, Patrick Besnier and Bernard Le Doze (Paris, 1972–1988), vol. I, p. 1038.

2 Unpublished letter from Charles Filiger to Jules Bois, June 1894, Bibliothèque du Musée départemental de Maurice Denis, Saint Germain-en-Laye.

3 Dorothy Menpes, *Brittany* (London, 1905), p. 138.

4 Cited in Estelle Fresneau, 'Hommage à Gauguin: trois poèmes de Jarry

offerts au musée de Pont-Aven', *303*, 95 (2007) p. 52.

5 *Œuvres complètes*, i, pp. 1024–8.

6 Marie-Françoise Quignard, ed., *Le Mercure de France cent ans d'édition* (Paris, 1995), p. 61.

7 Laurent de Freitas, 'Léon-Paul Fargue et Alfred Jarry autour d'une même passion pour la peinture: 1892–1894', *L'Étoile-Absinthe*, 103–4 (2003), p. 18.

8 *Cahiers du Collège de 'Pataphysique*, Dossier 22–4, pp. 14–18.

9 Menpes, *Brittany*, p. 141.

10 *Œuvres complètes*, i, p. 680.

11 Mira Jacob, *Filiger l'inconnu* (Strasbourg, 1990), p. 20.

12 Jacquelynn Baas and Richard Field, *The Artistic Revival of the Woodcut* (Ann Arbor, mi, 1984), p. 64, n. 2.

13 *Œuvres complètes*, i, pp. 1027–8.

14 Émile Bernard, 'Mémoire pour l'Histoire du Symbolisme en 1890', in Pierre Cailler, *Émile Bernard et ses amis* (Geneva, 1957).

15 *Œuvres complètes*, iii, p. 703.

16 Paul Leclercq, *Autour de Toulouse-Lautrec* (Paris, 1921).

17 Arthur Gold and Robert Fizdale, *Misia*: *The Life of Misia Sert* (London, 1980), p. 54.

18 Ben Fisher, 'Alfred Jarry and the Army: An Ambiguous Desertion', unpublished paper presented to the Société des Dix-neuviémistes conference, 2006.

19 *Œuvres complètes*, i, pp. 1041–2.

20 Rachilde, *Alfred Jarry ou le Surmâle des lettres* (Paris, 1928), p. 66.

21 Baas and Field, *Artistic Revival of the Woodcut*, p. 64.

22 Jill Fell, 'Alain Jans et Richart Gheym: Les artistes «inconnus» de *L'Ymagier*', in Patrick Besnier, ed., *Jarry, monstres et merveilles* (Rennes, 2007), pp. 99–110.

23 *L'Ymagier*, i (1894), p. 5.

24 *Œuvres complètes* i, p. 972.

25 Paul Gauguin, *Diverses Choses*, Louvre ms (c. 1896–7), p. 215.

26 Paul Fort, *Toute la vie d'un poète, 1872–1943* (Paris, 1944), p. 47.

27 *Œuvres complètes*, i, p. 680.

28 Henry Certigny, 'L'École de Pont-Aven et les Nabis', in Pierre Waleffe, *La Vie des grands peintres impressionnistes et Nabis* (Paris, 1964), p. 444.

29 André Salmon, *Souvenirs sans fin*, vol. i (Paris, 1955), pp. 152–3.

30 Henri Bordillon, *Gestes et opinions d'Alfred Jarry, écrivain* (Laval, 1986),

p. 63.

31 Noël Arnaud, *Alfred Jarry, d'Ubu roi au docteur Faustroll* (Paris, 1974),
p. 112.

32 Ibid.

33 Ibid., p. 91.

4 Military Service: Fiction and Fact

1 Besnier, *Alfred Jarry* (Paris, 2005), p. 171.

2 Géroy (pseudonym of Gaston Roig), 'Mon ami Alfred Jarry', *Mercure de France*, July 1947, p. 24, reprinted in *L'Étoile-Absinthe*, 59–60 (1993), p. 26.

3 Ibid., p. 33, also cited in Besnier, *Alfred Jarry*, p. 176.

4 Noël Arnaud, *Alfred Jarry, d'Ubu roi au docteur Faustroll* (Paris, 1974), p. 136.

5 Alfred Jarry, *Œuvres complètes*, ed. Michel Arrivé, Henri Bordillon, Patrick Besnier and Bernard Le Doze (Paris, 1972–1988), vol. I, p. 761.

6 Arnaud, *Alfred Jarry*, p. 147.

7 *Œuvres complètes*, I, pp. 751–2.

8 Ibid., III, p. 702.

9 Caroline Boyle-Turner, *Le Talisman, 1888*, in *Nabis 1888–1900*, exh. cat., Kunsthaus, Zürich, and Galeries nationales du Grand Palais (Paris, Munich and Zürich, 1993), p. 249.

10 Paul Gauguin, 'Natures mortes', *Essais d'art libre*, IV (1893–4), pp. 273–5.

11 *Œuvres complètes*, I, p. 778.

12 Nicholas Wadley, ed., *Noa Noa: Gauguin's Tahiti* (London, 1985), pp. 25–8.

13 *Œuvres complètes*, I, p. 748.

14 Ibid., I, p. 767.

15 Ibid., I, p. 768.

16 Henri Bordillon, 'Études jarryques', *Organographes du Collège de 'Pataphysique*, 6, pp. 83–5.

17 Besnier, *Alfred Jarry*, p. 257.

18 *Œuvres complètes*, I, pp. 749–50.

19 *Œuvres complètes*, I, pp. 811–2, and II, p. 508.

20 Arnaud, *Alfred Jarry*, p. 175.

21 Géroy in *L'Étoile-Absinthe*, 59–60 (1993), p. 33.

22 *Œuvres complètes*, I, p. 1042 and Michel Arrivé, *Peintures, Gravures & Dessins d'Alfred Jarry* (Paris, 1968).

23 Rachilde, *Alfred Jarry, ou le Surmâle des lettres* (Paris, 1928), p. 54.

24 Jean-Paul Goujon, *Jean de Tinan* (Paris, 1990), p. 183.

25 Rachilde, *Alfred Jarry*, p. 55.

26 Ibid., p. 56.

27 *Œuvres complètes*, I, p. 854.

28 Letter from Rachilde to Jarry published by Alain Mercier in *L'Étoile-Absinthe*, 46, p. 18 and reprinted in Patrick Besnier, ed., *Alfred Jarry*, p. 345.

29 *Mercure de France*, 16 November 1907, cited in Keith Beaumont, *Alfred Jarry. A Critical and Biographical Study* (Leicester, 1984), p. 293.

30 Jarry, 'Premier son de la Messe', *Perhinderion*, I (1896), n.p.

5 'After Us the Savage God'

1 Julien Schuh, '*César-Antechrist*, un écrin occulte pour Ubu', in Patrick Besnier, ed., *Jarry, monstres et merveilles* (Rennes, 2007), pp. 13–46.

2 Jacques Robichez, *Le Symbolisme au théâtre. Lugné-Poe et les débuts de l'Œuvre* (Paris, 1957), pp. 188–96.

3 Paul Fort, *Toute la vie d'un poète 1872–1943* (Paris, 1944), p. 47.

4 Noël Arnaud, *Alfred Jarry, d'Ubu roi au docteur Faustroll* (Paris, 1974), pp. 187–8.

5 Aurélien Lugné-Poe, *Acrobaties: Souvenirs et impressions de théâtre, 1894–1902* (Paris, 1930), pp. 160–70.

6 Alfred Jarry, *Œuvres complètes*, ed. Michel Arrivé, Henri Bordillon, Patrick Besnier and Bernard Le Doze (Paris, 1972–1988), vol. I, p. 1044.

7 Ibid., I, p. 1043.

8 Lugné-Poe, *Acrobaties*, p. 170.

9 *Répertoire de l'Œuvre* (Paris, 1929) and Fell, 'Les remaniements de Jarry au texte de *Peer Gynt*', *L'Étoile-Absinthe*, 79–80 (1998), pp. 24–5.

10 Lugné-Poe, *Acrobaties*, p. 174.

11 William Butler Yeats, *Autobiographies* (London, 1955), p. 349.

12 *Œuvres complètes*, I, p. 400.

13 Ibid., I, p. 1058.

14 Ibid., I, pp. 408–9.

15 Ibid., I, p. 409.

16 Ibid., i, p. 1050.

17 Arnaud, *Alfred Jarry*, pp. 222–4.

18 *Œuvres complètes*, i, p. 1056.

19 Keith Beaumont, *Jarry: Ubu Roi* (London, 1987), p. 42.

20 'Répertoire des costumes', *Œuvres complètes*, i, p. 403.

21 Yeats, *Autobiographies*, p. 349.

22 Arnaud, *Alfred Jarry*, pp. 254–5.

23 Arthur Symons, 'A Symbolist Farce', in *Studies in Seven Arts* (London, 1906), p. 373, and Robert Vallier, review in the *République Française*, cited in Arnaud, *Alfred Jarry*, p. 313.

24 Roger Shattuck, *The Banquet Years* (London, 1969), p. 206.

25 Romain Coolus, Review of *Ubu Roi* in *La Revue blanche*, 1 January 1897 reprinted in *Cahiers du Collège de 'Pataphysique*, 3–4, p. 75.

26 Firmin Gémier, Interview published in *Excelsior*, 4 November 1921, cited in Besnier, *Alfred Jarry*, p. 271.

27 Arnaud, *Alfred Jarry*, p. 314.

28 Ibid.

29 Georges Rémond, 'Souvenirs sur Jarry et quelques autres', *Mercure de France*, March–April, 1955, reprinted in Henri Béhar, *Jarry dramaturge* (Paris, 1980), p. 73.

30 *Cahiers du Collège de 'Pataphysique*, 3–4, p. 75.

31 Cited in Arnaud, *Alfred Jarry*, p. 316.

32 Letter of 27 October 1896, in Stéphane Mallarmé, *Correspondance*, ed. Henri Mondor and Lloyd James Austin (Paris, 1983), p. 256.

6 'The Rising Light of the Quartier Latin'?

1 Noël Arnaud, *Alfred Jarry, d'Ubu roi au docteur Faustroll* (Paris, 1974), p. 332, n. 1.

2 Patrick Besnier, *Alfred Jarry* (Paris, 2005), p. 289.

3 Ibid., p. 250.

4 'Variations sur un thème de Bosse de Nage', *Subsidia pataphysica*, 26, pp. 19–24.

5 Alfred Jarry, *Œuvres complètes*, ed. Michel Arrivé, Henri Bordillon, Patrick Besnier and Bernard Le Doze (Paris, 1972–1988), vol. i, p. 1056.

6 Carola Giedion-Welcker, *Poètes à l'écart/Anthologie der Abseitigen* (Zürich, 1946), pp. 5–7.

7 *Œuvres complètes*, II, p. 441.

8 Ibid., I, pp. 821–8.

9 *The Letters of Aubrey Beardsley*, ed. Henry Maas, J. L. Duncan and W. G. Good (London, 1971), p. 339.

10 Arnaud, *Alfred Jarry*, p. 398.

11 Letter postmarked 25 May 1898, in *The Complete Letters of Oscar Wilde*, ed. Merlin Holland and Rupert Hart-Davis (London, 2000), p. 1075.

12 Ben Fisher, *The Pataphysician's Library: An Exploration of Jarry's livres pairs* (Liverpool, 2000), p. 4.

13 *Jarry e la Patafisica*, exh. cat., Comune di Milano (Milan, 1983) p. 48, and exh. cat., Ivam Centre Julio Gonzalez, *Alfred Jarry, De los nabis a la patafisica* (Valencia, 2000), p. 65.

14 Jean Loize, 'Alfred Jarry, est-il le sourcier inconnu de l'art moderne?' *Beaux-arts, Spectacles, Théâtres* (6–10 July 1953), p. 11.

15 Jean Starobinski, *Portrait de l'artiste en saltimbanque* (Geneva, 1970), p. 9.

16 Brigid Brophy, *Beardsley and his World* (London, 1976), p. 99.

17 *Œuvres complètes*, I, p. 661.

18 Jill Fell, 'The Deceptive Images of Alfred Jarry: Lost, Found and Invented Portraits by Beardsley, Rousseau and Rippl-Ronaï', *Word & Image* XV/2 (1999), pp. 191–2.

19 *Œuvres complètes*, I, p. 678.

20 Vincent O'Sullivan, *Aspects of Wilde* (Toronto, 1936), p. 87.

21 *Œuvres complètes*, vol. II, p. 441.

22 Ibid., I, p. 953.

23 Ibid., p. 678. The emboldened words indicate falsity.

24 Oscar Wilde, *Salome* (New York, 1967), pp. 58–9.

25 *Œuvres complètes*, I, p. 665.

26 *The Book of the Thousand Nights and One Night*, vol. IV (London, 1947), p. 168.

27 *Œuvres complètes*, I, p. 677

28 Gauguin, *Diverses Choses*, Louvre MS (c. 1896–7), p. 218.

29 'Nécrologie', *Œuvres complètes*, I, pp. 564–5.

30 Arnaud, *Alfred Jarry*, p. 374.

31 Ibid.

32 Ibid., p. 378.

33 *Cahiers du Collège de 'Pataphysique*, 15, p. 21.

34 Philippe Cathé, *Claude Terrasse* (Paris, 2004), p. 49.

7 From Puppets to Pataphysics

1 Alfred Jarry, *Œuvres complètes*, ed. Michel Arrivé, Henri Bordillon, Patrick Besnier and Bernard Le Doze (Paris, 1972–1988), vol. I, p. 561.

2 Henri Bordillon, 'Ronde autour du Théâtre des Pantins', *L'Étoile-Absinthe* 29–30 (1986), pp. 5–27.

3 Henry Certigny, 'L'École de Pont-Aven et les Nabis', in Pierre Waleffe, *La Vie des grands peintres impressionnistes et Nabis* (Paris, 1964), p. 414.

4 Advertisement in the *Mercure de France*, December 1897, cited in Patrick Besnier, *Alfred Jarry* (Paris, 2005), p. 334, n. 6.

5 Besnier, *Alfred Jarry*, p. 333.

6 Jacques Robichez, *Le Symbolisme au théâtre. Lugné-Poe et les débuts de l'Œuvre* (Paris, 1957), pp. 394–5.

7 *Œuvres complètes*, I, pp. 422–3.

8 A.-Ferdinand Hérold, 'Claude Terrasse', *Mercure de France*, 1 August 1923, pp. 695–6.

9 Bordillon, 'Ronde autour du Théâtre des Pantins', p. 21.

10 Keith Beaumont, *Alfred Jarry: A Critical and Biographical Study* (Leicester, 1984), p. 143.

11 Besnier, *Alfred Jarry*, p. 342.

12 Alfred Jarry, *Ubu*, ed. Noel Arnaud and Henri Bordillon (Paris, 1978), p. 453.

13 Fragment published by Cathé, *L'Étoile-Absinthe*, 77–8 (1997), p. 178.

14 *Œuvres complètes*, I, pp. 1064–5.

15 Published in *Cahiers du Collège de 'Pataphysique*, 22–3, p. 54.

16 *The Complete Letters of Oscar Wilde*, ed. Merlin Holland and Rupert Hart-Davis (London, 2000), p. 1070.

17 *Cahiers du Collège de 'Pataphysique*, 8–9, p. 75.

18 *Complete Letters of Oscar Wilde*, p. 1075.

19 Noël Arnaud, *Alfred Jarry, d'Ubu roi au docteur Faustroll* (Paris, 1974), p. 418.

20 *Œuvres complètes*, II, pp. 488–91.

21 Ibid., pp. 362–3.

22 Misia Sert, *Souvenirs*, cited in Patrick Besnier, *Alfred Jarry*, p. 353.

23 Ibid., cited in Arthur Gold and Robert Fizdale, *Misia: The Life of Misia Sert* (London, 1980), p. 58.

24 Cited in Arnaud, *Alfred Jarry*, p. 240.

25 *Œuvres complètes*, I, p. 1298.

26 Ibid., I, pp. 564–5.

27 Fernand Lot, *Alfred Jarry* (Paris, 1934), p. 33.

28 Cf. Fisher, *The Pataphysician's Library* and Patrick Besnier, *Alfred Jarry* (Paris, 1990).

29 *Œuvres complètes*, II, pp. 432–5.

30 Henri Bordillon, *Gestes et opinions d'Alfred Jarry, écrivain* (Laval, 1986), p. 174.

31 Fisher, *The Pataphysician's Library*, p. 7.

32 *Œuvres complètes*, I, p. 702.

33 Cf. Besnier, *Alfred Jarry*, pp. 388–91.

34 *Œuvres complètes* I, p. 668.

35 Ibid., I, p. 249.

36 Isabelle Kzrywkowski, 'Les "13" images', in *Alfred Jarry et les Arts* (Paris and Tusson, 2007), pp. 129–38.

37 *Œuvres complètes*, I, p. 716.

38 Ibid., p. 717.

39 Letter from Charles Morin cited in Charles Chassé, *Sous le masque d'Alfred Jarry. Les Sources d'Ubu-Roi* (Paris, 1921), p. 35.

40 *Œuvres complètes*, I, p. 181.

41 Ibid., p. 172.

42 Édouard Dujardin, 'Au xx et aux Indépendants: Le Cloisonisme [sic]', *La Revue indépendante*, 17 (1888), pp. 487–92, extract reprinted in 'D'Art', *Perhinderion*, 2 (Paris, 1896). Jarry attributed the piece to Félix Fénéon, in whose *Calendrier* it appeared.

43 Besnier, *Alfred Jarry*, p. 367.

44 Beaumont's translation in his *Alfred Jarry*, p. 195.

45 *Œuvres complètes*, vol. II, p. 434.

46 Ibid., vol. I, p. 668.

47 Ibid., p. 1072.

8 Through the Dimensions

1 Rachilde, *Alfred Jarry, ou le Surmâle des lettres* (Paris, 1928), p. 136.

2 *Jarry. Autour d'un testament*, exh. cat. Archives départementales de la Mayenne (Laval, 2007), p. 15.

3 Brunella Eruli, *Jarry. I Mostri dell'immagine* (Pisa, 1982), pp. 152–66.

4 Alfred Jarry, *Œuvres complètes*, ed. Michel Arrivé, Henri Bordillon, Patrick Besnier and Bernard Le Doze (Paris, 1972–1988), I, p. 1075.

5 Keith Beaumont, *Alfred Jarry: A Critical and Biographical Study* (Leicester, 1984), p. 168.

6 *Cahiers du Collège de 'Pataphysique*, 8–9, p. 75.

7 *Œuvres complètes*, III, pp. 593–4.

8 Ibid., I, p. 921.

9 Carola Giedion-Welcker, *Alfred Jarry* (Zürich, 1960), p. 81.

10 *Œuvres complètes*, I, p. 957.

11 Beaumont, *Alfred Jarry*, p. 177.

12 Letter of 9 January 1899 cited in Patrick Besnier, *Alfred Jarry* (Paris, 2005), pp. 384–5.

13 Jean Loize, 'La Grande Chasublerie d'Alfred Jarry', *Cahiers du Collège de 'Pataphysique*, 5–6 (1952), p. 67.

14 *Œuvres complètes*, I, pp. 1073–4.

15 Rachilde, *Alfred Jarry*, pp. 164–5.

16 Jean-Paul Goujon, *Pierre Louÿs* (Paris, 2002), p. 594.

17 *Œuvres complètes*, II, p. 119.

18 Ibid., II, p. 107.

19 Ibid., II, p. 109.

20 Jill Fell, *Alfred Jarry: An Imagination in Revolt* (Madison, Teaneck, NJ, 2005), pp. 180–81.

21 Richard Ellmann, *Oscar Wilde* (London, 1988), p. 209.

22 *Œuvres complètes*, II, pp. 331–6.

9 Journalism, *Le Surmâle* and Brussels

1 Philippe Régibier, *Ubu sur la berge* (Paris, 1999), p. 100.

2 Rachilde, *Alfred Jarry, ou le Surmâle des lettres* (Paris, 1928), pp. 187–9.

3 Alfred Jarry, *Œuvres complètes*, ed. Michel Arrivé, Henri Bordillon, Patrick Besnier and Bernard Le Doze (Paris, 1972–1988), II, pp. 432–5.

4 Ibid., II, pp. 420–22, and *Selected Works of Alfred Jarry*, ed. Roger Shattuck and Simon Watson-Taylor (London, 1965), pp. 122–4.

5 *Œuvres complètes*, III, p. 564.

6 'De quelques animaux nuisibles: le volant', *Œuvres complètes*, II, pp. 351–2.

7 'Les mœurs des noyés', *Œuvres complètes*, II, pp. 357–8.

8 'Cynégétique de l'omnibus', *Œuvres complètes*, II, pp. 328–30.

9 *Œuvres complètes*, II, pp. 640–41.

10 Ibid., II p. 360.

11 Ibid., II pp. 275–6.

12 Ibid., II pp. 287–8.

13 André Fontainas, *De Mallarmé à Paul Valéry. Notes d'un témoin* (Paris, 1928), n.p.

14 *Œuvres complètes*, vol. I, pp. 185–7.

15 Ibid., II, p. 270.

16 Ibid., p. 361.

17 Ibid., pp. 393–4.

18 *Mercure de France* (16 November 1907), cited in Keith Beaumont, *Alfred Jarry: A Critical and Biographical Study* (Leicester, 1984), pp. 292–3.

19 *Œuvres complètes*, II, p. 206.

20 Ibid., II, p. 189, and *The Supermale*, trans. Barbara Wright (London, 1951), p. 7.

21 Ibid., II, pp. 262–3.

22 Ibid., II, p. 338.

23 Omer-Désiré Bothey, *Introduction* to *Ubu sur la Butte*, in Alfred Jarry, *Œuvres* (Paris, 2004), pp. 369–71.

24 Barbara Pascarel, *Ubu roi – Ubu cocu – Ubu enchaîné – Ubu sur la Butte d'Alfred Jarry* (Paris, 2008), p. 170.

25 Sander Pierron,'Alfred Jarry à Bruxelles', *Mercure de France*, 1 November 1931, pp. 718–27.

26 Besnier, *Alfred Jarry* (Paris, 2005), p. 484, n. 19.

27 *Œuvres complètes*, II, p. 643.

28 L. Dumont-Wilden, 'Souvenirs du Père Ubu', *Le Soir*, 10 November 1937.

29 *Mercure de France*, June 1902, pp. 836–7, cited in Besnier, *Alfred Jarry*, p. 489.

30 *Œuvres complètes*, II, pp. 584–5.

31 Ibid., I, p. 1171, n. 4.

10 Poverty, Illness and Death

1 Alfred Jarry, *Œuvres*, ed. Michel Décaudin (Paris, 2004), pp. 1147–8.

2 Charles-Albert Cingria, cited in Patrick Besnier, *Alfred Jarry* (Paris, 2005), p. 605, n. 23.

3 John Richardson, *A Life of Picasso*, vol. I (London, 1991), p. 366.

4 Guillaume Apollinaire, *Journal intime*, cited in Besnier, *Alfred Jarry*, p. 527.

5 Henri Bordillon, *Gestes et opinions d'Alfred Jarry, écrivain* (Laval, 1986), p. 202.

6 Alfred Jarry, *Œuvres complètes*, ed. Michel Arrivé, Henri Bordillon, Patrick Besnier and Bernard Le Doze (Paris, 1972–1988), vol. III, p. 455.

7 Josep Palau i Fabre, *Picasso en Catalunia* (Barcelona, 1966), p. 165, cited in John Richardson, *A Life of Picasso*, vol. I, p. 364 and vol. II, p. 126.

8 Guillaume Apollinaire, *Œuvres en prose complètes* (Paris, 1977–93), vol. IV, pp. 423–44.

9 Ibid., II, pp. 1038–9.

10 F. T. Marinetti, *Selected Writings*, trans. R. W. Flint and Arthur A. Coppotelli, (London, 1972), p. 330.

11 *Œuvres complètes*, III, pp. 635–6.

12 Ibid., I, p. 972.

13 Ibid., III, p. 585.

14 Cathé, 'Alfred Jarry and Music', trans. Elizabeth Power, in exh. cat., Ivam Centre Julio Gonzalez, *Alfred Jarry, De los nabis a la patafisica*, (Valencia, 2000), p. 203.

15 J.-H. Sainmont, 'L'interminable histoire du *Pantagruel*', *Cahiers du Collège de 'Pataphysique*, 15 (1954), p. 27–8.

16 Fernand Lot, *Alfred Jarry. Son Œuvre* (Paris, 1934), p. 35.

17 Bordillon, *Gestes et opinions d'Alfred Jarry*, p. 125.

18 Noël Arnaud Archive, cited in Besnier, *Alfred Jarry*, p. 574.

19 Cathé, 'Alfred Jarry and Music', p. 202.

20 Bordillon, *Gestes et opinions d'Alfred Jarry*, p. 127.

21 Stéphen-Chauvet, 'Les derniers jours d'Alfred Jarry', *L'Étoile-Absinthe*, 67–8 (1995), p. 30.

22 *Œuvres complètes*, III, pp.461–94.

23 Sylvain-Christian David, *Introduction* to *La Dragonne*, in Jarry, *Œuvres*, p. 1133.

24 See *Œuvres complètes*, II, p. 545 for the whole poem.

25 Rachilde, *Alfred Jarry, ou le Surmâle des lettres* (Paris, 1928), p. 180.

26 *Œuvres complètes*, III, p. 454.

27 Jean Saltas, 'Souvenirs sur Alfred Jarry', *L'Étoile-Absinthe*, 51–52 (1992), pp. 25–9.

28 *Œuvres complètes*, III, p. 627.

29 Ibid., III, p. 615.

30 Bordillon, *Gestes et opinions d'Alfred Jarry*, p. 186.

31 *Œuvres complètes*, III, p. 613.

32 Ibid., III, p. 614.

33 Ibid., III, pp. 616–17.

34 Ibid., III, p. 627.

35 *Organographes du Cymbalum pataphysicum*, 18 (1982), p. 19.

36 *Œuvres complètes*, III, p. 625.

37 Ibid., III, pp. 622–3.

38 Ibid., III, p. 980.

39 Bordillon, *Gestes et opinions d'Alfred Jarry*, p. 172.

40 *Œuvres complètes* III, p. 655.

41 Ibid., III, p. 661.

42 Ibid., III, pp. 684–5.

43 Ibid., III, p. 1007–8.

44 Stéphen-Chauvet, 'Les derniers jours d'Alfred Jarry', pp. 32–3.

45 *Œuvres complètes*, III, p. 695.

46 Ibid., III, p. 1012.

47 Stéphen-Chauvet, 'Les derniers jours d'Alfred Jarry', pp. 26–7.

48 Bordillon, *Gestes et opinions d'Alfred Jarry*, p. 193.

49 Apollinaire, *Œuvres en prose complètes*, vol. II, p. 1043.

Epilogue

1 Stéphen-Chauvet, 'Les derniers jours d'Alfred Jarry', *L'Étoile-Absinthe*, 67–8 (1995), pp. 32–3.

2 Guillaume Apollinaire, *Œuvres en prose complètes* (Paris, 1977–93), vol. II, p. 1044.

Bibliography

Works

For all quotations I have used the Pléiade edition of Jarry's *Œuvres complètes* in three volumes edited and annotated by Michel Arrivé, Henri Bordillon, Patrick Besnier and Bernard Le Doze (1972–1988). The Bouquins *Alfred Jarry. Œuvres* (2004) edited by Michel Décaudin is more chronologically correct and contains the most authentic version of *La Dragonne,* but lacks most of Jarry's letters and Charlotte Jarry's *Notes.* I have referred to its commentaries. I have also referred to commentaries in the following editions:

Arnaud, Noël and Henri Bordillon, eds, *Ubu* (Paris, 1978)
Arnaud, Noël, ed., *Le Manoir enchanté et quatre autres inédits* (Paris, 1974)
Saillet, Maurice, ed., *La Chandelle verte* (Paris,1969)
Saillet, Maurice ed., *Tout Ubu* (Paris, 1962)
Messaline, with a preface and notes by Thieri Foulc (Paris, 1977)
Le Surmâle, with a preface and notes by Thieri Foulc (Paris, 1977)

The publications of the Collège de 'Pataphysique contain invaluable material collected on Jarry since 1950. The journal *L'Étoile-Absinthe* published by the Société des Amis d'Alfred Jarry since 1979 specializes in recent and current research into Jarry's work by academics and others. It has published exhibition catalogues devoted to Jarry and reprinted articles that are otherwise hard to find.

Useful English editions

Ubu Roi, trans. Barbara Wright (London, 1951)
The Ubu Plays, trans. Cyril Connolly and Simon Watson-Taylor (New York, 1968)
Selected Works of Alfred Jarry, ed. Roger Shattuck and Simon Watson-Taylor (London, 1965)
The Supermale, trans. Barbara Wright (London, 1968)
Messalina, trans. John Harman (London, 1985)
Days and Nights, trans. Alexis Lykiard and Stanley Chapman, with *The Other Alcestis*, trans. John Harman (London, 1989)
Caesar Antichrist, trans. Anthony Melville (London, 1992)
Visits of Love, trans. Iain White (London, 1993)
Collected Works of Alfred Jarry, vols I and II, trans. Paul Edwards, Anthony Melville, Alexis Lykiard and Simon Watson-Taylor (London, 2001 and 2006)

Biographies

Arnaud, Noël, *Alfred Jarry, d'Ubu roi au docteur Faustroll* (Paris, 1974)
Beaumont, Keith, *Alfred Jarry: A Critical and Biographical Study* (Leicester, 1984)
Besnier, Patrick, *Alfred Jarry* (Paris, 2005)
Bordillon, Henri, *Gestes et opinions d'Alfred Jarry, écrivain* (Laval, 1986)
Lot, Fernand, *Alfred Jarry. Son Œuvre* (Paris, 1934)
Rachilde, *Alfred Jarry, ou le Surmâle des lettres* (Paris, 1928)
Régibier, Philippe, *Ubu sur la berge*: *Alfred Jarry à Corbeil (1899–1907)* (Paris, 1999)
Shattuck, Roger, *The Banquet Years: The Origins of the avant-garde in France, 1885 to World War I* (London, 1969)

Criticism

Arrivé, Michel, *Les Langages de Jarry. Essai de sémiotique littéraire* (Paris, 1972)
——, *Peintures, Gravures et Dessins d'Alfred Jarry* (Paris, 1968)

214

Béhar, Henri, *Jarry dramaturge* (Paris, 1980),
——, *La Dramaturgie d'Alfred Jarry* (Paris, 2003)
——, *Les Cultures de Jarry* (Paris, 1988)
Beaumont, Keith, *Jarry: Ubu Roi* (London, 1987)
Besnier, Patrick, *Alfred Jarry* (Paris, 1990)
Caradec, François, *A la recherche d'Alfred Jarry* (Paris, 1974)
Eruli, Brunella, *Jarry. I Mostri dell'Immagine* (Pisa, 1982)
Fell, Jill, *Alfred Jarry: An Imagination in Revolt* (Madison, Teaneck, NJ, 2005)
Fisher, Ben, *The Pataphysician's Library: An Exploration of Jarry's livres pairs*
    (Liverpool, 2000)
Giedion-Welcker, Carola, *Alfred Jarry* (Zürich, 1960)
Levesque, Jacques-Henry, *Alfred Jarry* (Paris, 1951)
Lugné-Poe, Aurélien, *Acrobaties: Souvenirs et impressions de théâtre, 1894–1902*
    (Paris, 1930)
Pascarel, Barbara, *Ubu roi – Ubu cocu – Ubu enchaîné – Ubu sur la Butte*
    d'Alfred Jarry (Paris, 2008)
Robichez, Jacques, *Le Symbolisme au théâtre. Lugné-Poe et les débuts de l'œuvre*
    (Paris, 1957)
Stillmann, Linda Klieger, *Alfred Jarry* (New York, 1984)
Van Schoonbeek, Christine, *Les Portraits d'Ubu* (Biarritz, 1997)

Special Issues

The following special issues of journals and conference papers have been
devoted to Jarry's work:

Europe, issue 623–4 (Paris, 1981)
L'Esprit créateur, issue 24/4 (Minnesota, 1984)
Colloque de Cérisy, Alfred Jarry (Paris, 1985)
La Revue des Sciences Humaines, 203 (Paris, 1986)
Magazine littéraire (La Pataphysique), issue 388 (Paris, 2000)
303, issue 95 (Nantes, 2007)
La Licorne, issue 80 (Poitiers, 2007)
Les Nouveaux Cahiers de la Comédie-Française (Paris, 2009)

Exhibition catalogues

Jarry e la Patafisica, exh. cat., Comune di Milano (Milan, 1983)

Alfred Jarry (1873–1907), exh. cat., Kunsthaus, Zürich (Zürich, 1984)

Ubu, cent ans de règne, exh. cat., Musée Galerie de la Seita and Société des amis d'Alfred Jarry (Paris, 1989)

Nabis 1888–1900, exh. cat., Kunsthaus, Zürich, and Galeries Nationales du Grand Palais (Paris, Munich and Zürich, 1993)

Ubu à l'Anvers, exh. cat., Galerie Ronny Van de Velde (Antwerp, 1997)

Ubu's Almanac: Alfred Jarry and the Graphic Arts, exh. cat., Spencer Museum of Art (Lawrence, Kansas, 1998)

Alfred Jarry. De los nabis a la patafisica, exh. cat., Ivam Centre Julio Gonzalez (Valencia, 2000)

Le Théâtre de l'Œuvre, 1893–1900, exh. cat., Musée d'Orsay (Paris, 2005)

Jarry. Autour d'un testament, exh. cat., Archives départementales de la Mayenne (Laval, 2007)

Acknowledgements

I should like to thank Patrick Besnier, Thieri Foulc, Henri Béhar, Michel Arrivé, Phillippe Cathé, Sylvain-Christian David, Paul Edwards, Olivier Michaud, Dominique Remande, Julien Schuh, Lejla Haveric, Edouard Sébline, Maria Gonzales Menendez, Marie El Caïdi, Sylvie Fresnault, Linda Stillman, Belinda Thomson and Caroline Boyle-Turner for responding to my questions. Nick Wadley, Liz Drew and Gregory Edwards helped me with illustrations. William Fell and Joanna Woods were my patient readers and critics. I am indebted to Patrick Fréchet for generously allowing me to publish photographs and illustrations from his archive, without which this book would not have been possible in its present form.

Photo Acknowledgements

The author and publishers wish to express their thanks to the below sources of illustrative material and/or permission to reproduce it. Locations of some artworks are also given below.

© ADAGP, Paris and DACS, London 2010: p. 9; collection of the artist (Ossip Zadkine): p. 9; reprinted from *Étoile-Absinthe*, nos. 17–18 (1983): p. 121; reprinted from *Étoile-Absinthe*, nos. 93–4 (2002): pp. 73, 104; reprinted from *Étoile-Absinthe* (nos 109–10, 2006): pp. 55, 56; Patrick Fréchet collection: pp. 6, 21, 23, 24, 30, 35, 66, 92, 98, 102, 124, 152, 188, 189; reproduced courtesy of Patrick Fréchet: p. 68; from Remy de Gourmont, *Le IIe Livre des Masques* (Paris, 1898): pp. 31, 34; Harvard Art Museum, Fogg Art Museum, Cambridge, MA (bequest of Scofield Thayer – photo Imaging Department © President and Fellows of Harvard College): p. 106; Musée des Arts et Traditions Populaires, Paris (photo © F. Duchesne/RMN): p. 168; photo © Musée de Pont-Aven: p. 44; reproduced from *Peintures, Gravures & Dessins d'Alfred Jarry*, ed. Michel Arrivé (Paris: Collège de 'Pataphysique, 1968): pp. 38, 41, 77, 86, 105; private collections: pp. 42, 117, 139, 144, 167; reproduced in *Revue blanche*, 13e année, XXVIII/215 (15 May 1902): p. 167; photo Routhier, Studio Lourmel and Musée Maurice Denis, Saint-Germain-en-Laye: p. 46; courtesy Société des Amis d'Alfred Jarry: pp. 55, 56, 73, 104, 121; © Succession Picasso/DACS 2010: p. 172; photo Marc Vaux: p. 9; courtesy Victoria and Albert Museum, London: p. 44; courtesy Alain Weill: p. 120.